NORWEGIAN SWEATERS AND JACKETS

KARI HESTNES

NORWEGIAN SWEATERS AND JACKETS

✵ 37 STUNNING SCANDINAVIAN PATTERNS ✵

Trafalgar Square
North Pomfret, Vermont

First published in the United States of America
in 2022 by
Trafalgar Square Books
North Pomfret, Vermont

Originally published in Norwegian as *Strikk mine fineste skatter*.

Copyright © Gyldendal Norsk Forlag AS, Oslo 2020
English translation © 2022 Trafalgar Square Books

All rights reserved. No part of this book may be reproduced, by any means, without written permission of the publisher, except by a reviewer quoting brief excerpts for a review in a magazine, newspaper or website.

The instructions and material lists in this book were carefully reviewed by the author and editor; however, accuracy cannot be guaranteed. The author and publisher cannot be held liable for errors.

ISBN: 978-1-64601-142-1
Library of Congress Control Number: 2022934258

Interior design: Lise Mosveen
Photography: Kari Hestnes
Portrait photo on page 5 and cover: Aleksander Stav
Professional consultant: May-Britt Bjella Zamori
Translation into English: Carol Huebscher Rhoades
Cover design: RM Didier

Printed in China
10 9 8 7 6 5 4 3 2 1

TABLE OF CONTENTS

Preface	5
Suzanna	7
Inti	12
French Lily	16
Hope	21
Oasis	27
Butterfly in Winterland	31
Myra	40
Leaf	44
Inanna	48
Glastonbury	53
Frida's Mexican Jacket	58
Bonbon	64
Rosita	68
Morning Red	75
Golden Days	78
Oline	85
Tumi	88
Queen of Diamonds	92
Sunflower	98
Klara	102
Vanda	106
Spring Shoots	112
Zephyr	116
Queen of Hearts	120
Apple Blossom	124
Frida's Midsummer Jacket	128
Drops Cardigan	134
Delft	139
Hagia Sophia	143
Olivia	147
Conifer Forest	152
Talia	157
Late Autumn	160
Filippa	164
Lilli	171
Winter Poetry	174
Amanda	181
Yarn Resources and Abbreviations	184
Acknowledgments	185

PREFACE

Welcome to my creative universe. Knitting has been my passion, my hobby, and my work for almost 40 years, and even after all that time, new colors, exciting knitting techniques, and lovely yarn are still so exciting. The possibilities are endless.

I find inspiration in so many ways—but for me, all of them are about being present. Having time to observe, to enjoy, to take in what is around me. Often, I'm inspired by my travels, both inside Norway and abroad, including my daily walks, and every time I take out the camera and focus myself on the small details in nature. Photography is a way to be present, for me, and when I am in a beautiful place, fully experiencing the moment, that's when inspiration comes. That's why I've chosen to illustrate each design in this book with one or more of my photographs, so you can also be inspired.

In *Norwegian Sweaters and Jackets*, I've taken a deep dive into my treasure chest and brought out some of my most popular designs: 37 gorgeous, timeless jackets and sweaters, comfortable as everyday wear and at the same time elegant enough for special occasions. In this book, you'll find pattern-knitted cardigans, classic cable pullovers, and delicate lace knitting in the most beautiful yarns. Use your imagination, choose your own colors, and put your personal touch on the garments.

Do you want to see more of my designs? Head over to my webpage: www.karihdesign.com.

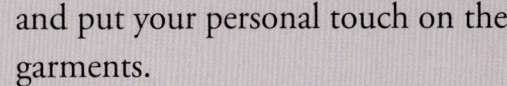

SUZANNA

CARDIGAN WITH ROUND YOKE

Suzanna is one of my most popular designs. This cardigan has a round yoke with colorful panels, narrow ribbed edgings, and crocheted front bands.

SKILL LEVEL
Intermediate to Experienced

SIZES
S (M, L, XL, XXL)

FINISHED MEASUREMENTS
Chest: 35½ (38½, 41¾, 48¾, 54¼) in / 90 (98, 106, 124, 138) cm
Total Length: 24½ (24¾, 25¼, 26, 26¾) in / 62 (63, 64, 66, 68) cm
Sleeve Length: 19 (19, 19¼, 19¼, 19¼) in / 48 (48, 49, 49, 49) cm

MATERIALS
Yarn:
CYCA #2 (sport, baby) Hillesvåg Ask/Hifa 2 (100% Norwegian wool, 344 yd/315 m / 100 g)

Yarn Colors and Amounts:
Color 1: Orange Heather 6570: 300 (350, 350, 400, 450) g
Color 2: Black 6053: 50 (100, 100, 100, 100) g
Color 3: Lime-Green 6113: 50 (50, 50, 50, 50) g
Color 4: Brown 6141: 50 (50, 50, 50, 50) g
Color 5: Sea-Green 6029: 50 (50, 50, 50, 50) g
Color 6: Ochre 6133: 50 (50, 50, 50, 50) g
Needles: U. S. sizes 1.5 and 2.5 / 2.5 and 3 mm circulars and sets of 5 dpn.
If you work two-color stranded knitting more tightly than single-color knitting, use U. S. 4 / 3.5 mm for those sections.
Crochet Hook: U. S. B-1 or C-2 / 2.5 mm
Notions: 10 buttons to match colors in cardigan. Approx. 1.6 yd / 1.5 m of ribbon to cover cut edges of steek.

GAUGE
24 sts in stockinette/pattern with U. S. 2.5 / 3 mm or pattern with U. S. 4 / 3.5 mm = 4 in / 10 cm.
Adjust needle size to obtain correct gauge if necessary.

BODY

With smaller circular and Color 1, CO 217 (235, 255, 297, 331) sts + 6 sts at center front for steek.

Steek: Purl steek sts; do not include steek sts in stitch counts. To make later cutting and sewing easier, and to secure the yarns, work the 2 center sts in pattern color.

Knit 1 row (on WS). Turn and join, being careful not to twist cast-on row; pm for beginning of rnd.

Twisted Ribbing at Lower Edge: K2 (3, 1, 2, 3) tbl and then *p1, k3tbl*; rep * to * until 3 (0, 2, 3, 0) sts rem, p1 (0, 1, 1, 0), k2 (0, 1, 2, 0) tbl. Work a total of 8 rnds in ribbing as est. Change to larger circular and stockinette. Continuing with Color 1, work around until body measures 15½ in / 39 cm. Pm at each side with 54 (58, 63, 73, 82) sts for each front, making sure steek is centered on front, and 109 (119, 129, 151, 167) sts for back.

Shape Armholes: BO 12 (12, 12, 12, 14) sts at each side: BO 6 (6, 6, 6, 7) sts, knit until 6 (6, 6, 6, 7) sts before next side marker, BO 12 (12, 12, 12, 14) sts, knit until 6 (6, 6, 6, 7) sts before next marker, BO 6 (6, 6, 6, 7) sts. Set body aside.

SLEEVES

Work in the round. With smaller dpn and Color 2, CO 52 (52, 56, 60, 64) sts. Divide sts onto dpn and join. Work 8 rnds in k3tbl, p1 ribbing. Change to larger dpn (U. S. 4 / 3.5 mm) if you knit colorwork tightly—do so for all colorwork sections. Work around in pattern following Chart II for 1 repeat in length. See arrow for center of sleeve. Count out to determine where to begin the pattern for your size. After completing pattern, change to Color 1 and larger dpn for single-color stockinette. *At the same time:*

Shape Sleeve: On every 8th rnd, increase 2 sts centered on underarm until there are 80 (88, 96, 104, 116) sts. Continue without further increasing until sleeve is 19 (19, 19¼, 19¼, 19¼) in / 48 (48, 49, 49, 49) cm long.

Shape Armhole: BO 6 (6, 6, 6, 7) sts, knit until 6 (6, 6, 6, 7) sts rem and BO rem sts.

Set first sleeve aside and make second sleeve the same way.

JOINING BODY AND SLEEVES

Place all pieces on larger circular: front, right sleeve, back, left sleeve = 329 (363, 399, 457, 507) sts total. Pm at each intersection of body and sleeve = 4 markers. With Color 1, knit rnd, decreasing 8 (10, 6, 8, 10) sts evenly spaced around = 321 (353, 393, 449, 497) sts rem.

Raglan Shaping: Knit until 2 sts before first marker, k2tog tbl, sl m, k2tog. Decrease the same way at each marker. Decrease the same way on every rnd 2 (4, 5, 6, 8) times = 305 (321, 353, 401, 433) sts rem.

Yoke Pattern: End raglan shaping—remaining decreases are worked into pattern. Change to larger needle for colorwork if necessary. Work following Chart I with 19 (20, 22, 25, 27) rep around + 1st st on chart so pattern is symmetrical at center front). Continue in pattern to top of chart = 115 (121, 133, 151, 163) sts rem. BO rem sts.

FINISHING

Weave in all ends neatly on WS. Gently steam press on WS under damp pressing cloth. Machine-stitch 2 lines, zigzag and straight stitch, on each side of center front sts. Carefully cut open up center of steek. Seam underarms.

Front Bands and Neckband: Fold steek to WS. Beginning at lower edge of right front, with crochet hook and Color 2, work in sc into folded edge with 2 sc in corner. Work up right front, 2 sc in corner, around neck, 2 sc in corner, down left front edge. Turn, change to Color 6 and work 1 row sc.

Buttonhole Row: Mark spacing for 10 buttons, evenly spaced on right front band. Turn and work 1 row sc with Color 5, *at the same time* making each button loop: ch 4, skip 3 sc and work 1 sc in next sc. Turn, change to Color 3 and work 1 row sc, with 3 sc in each ch-4 loop.

Turn and change to Color 4; work 1 row sc.

Turn and change to Color 2; work 1 row sc.

Cut yarn and draw end through last loop; tighten and fasten off. Weave all ends neatly on WS.

Sew buttons onto left front band to match spacing of buttonholes. Sew ribbon on WS to cover cut steek edges.

CHART I

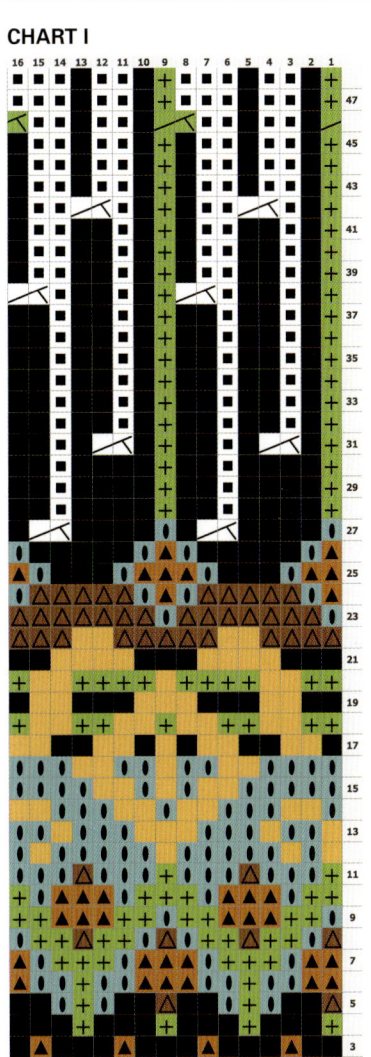

1 repeat = 16 sts

CHART II

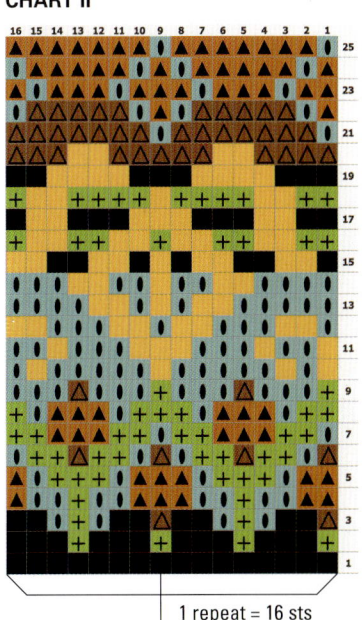

1 repeat = 16 sts

Center of sleeve

Symbols Key

- ▲ Color 1
- ■ Color 2
- ✚ Color 3
- ▲ Color 4
- ◗ Color 5
- ▢ Color 6
- ⟋ K2tog with Color 2
- ⟋ K2tog with Color 3
- ▪ No stitch—stitch has been decreased away

INTI

"Inti" is the name of the Incan sun god. This sweater is shaped to form a dressy A-line, with a stylized floral motif at the lower edges of the body and sleeves— a motif that's repeated around the rounded yoke.

SKILL LEVEL
Intermediate

SIZES
S/M (L/XL, XXL)

FINISHED MEASUREMENTS
Chest: 40¼ (47, 53½) in / 102 (119, 136) cm
Total Length: 27¼ (28, 28¾) in / 69 (71, 73) cm
Sleeve Length: 18½ (19, 19¼) in / 47 (48, 49) cm

MATERIALS
Yarn:
CYCA #1 (light fingering) Naturally Yarns New Zealand Amuri 4-ply (75% Merino wool, 25% possum, 262 yd/240 m / 50 g)
Yarn Colors and Amounts:
Red Heather 4026: 350 (400, 450) g
Needles: U. S. sizes 2.5 and 4 / 3 and 3.5 mm circulars and sets of 5 dpn

GAUGE
26 sts in stockinette with larger needles = 4 in / 10 cm.
Adjust needle size to obtain correct gauge if necessary

BODY

Lower Edges: The front and back edges are first worked separately. With smaller circular, CO 133 (155, 177) sts. Knit 4 rows back and forth. Work pattern following Chart I: Begin with first 11 sts, work repeat over next 110 (132, 154) sts = 5 (6, 7) rep, and end with the last 12 sts. Work 1 rep in length. Set piece aside and make a second edge the same way.

Joining, Body: Place both lower edges on larger circular and join; pm for beginning of rnd. Work around in stockinette until body measures 19¾ (20, 20) in / 50 (51, 51) cm. Pm at each side.

Shape Armholes: BO 10 sts at each side as follows: BO 5 sts, knit until 5 sts before next side marker, BO 10 sts, knit until 5 sts rem on rnd, BO rem 5 sts. Set body aside.

SLEEVES

The lower edge is worked back and forth and then continued in the round. With smaller dpn, CO 67 (67, 67) sts. Knit 4 rows back and forth. Work pattern following Chart I: Begin with first 11 sts, work 22-st repeat 2 times, and end with the last 12 sts on chart. Work 1 rep in length. Join to work in the round, change to larger needles, and begin working around in stockinette. On first rnd, increase 4 (8, 12) sts evenly spaced around = 71 (75, 79) sts.

Shape Sleeve: Increase 2 sts centered on underarm every 8th rnd until there are 99 (109, 121) sts. Continue without further shaping until sleeve is 18½ (19, 19¼) in / 47 (48, 49) cm long.

Armhole: BO 5 sts, knit until 5 sts rem, BO 5 sts. Set first sleeve aside and make second sleeve the same way.

JOINING BODY AND SLEEVES

Place all pieces on larger circular: front, right sleeve, back, left sleeve = 424 (488, 556) sts total. Pm at each intersection of body and sleeve = 4 markers. Knit 2 rnds without decreasing.

Raglan Shaping: Knit until 2 sts before first marker; k2tog tbl, sl m, k2tog. Decrease the same way at each marker. Decrease the same way on every rnd 5 (7, 8) times = 384 (432, 492) sts rem. Now decrease as est on every other rnd a total of 14 (17, 20) times = 272 (296, 332) sts rem. Knit 1 rnd, decreasing 7 (9, 1) sts evenly spaced around = 265 (287, 331) sts rem. Change to smaller circular and work in pattern following Chart II. Begin by working first 11 sts on chart, work rep 11 (12, 14) times, and end with last 12 sts on chart. Work 1 rep in length. Decreases are worked in pattern. After completing rep, 145 (157, 181) sts rem. Knit 1 rnd, decreasing 10 (10, 20) sts evenly spaced around = 135 (147, 161) sts rem. Knit 8 rnds in stockinette and then BO.

FINISHING

Weave in all ends neatly on WS. Gently steam press on WS under damp pressing cloth. Seam lower edges of body and sleeves and seam underarms.

Symbols Key

	Knit on RS, purl on WS
◢	K2tog
○	Yo
■	No stitch—stitch has been decreased away or is not in work
ǀ	K1tbl
◥	K2tog tbl
•	Purl on RS, knit on WS
▲	Sl 1, k2tog, psso

CHART I

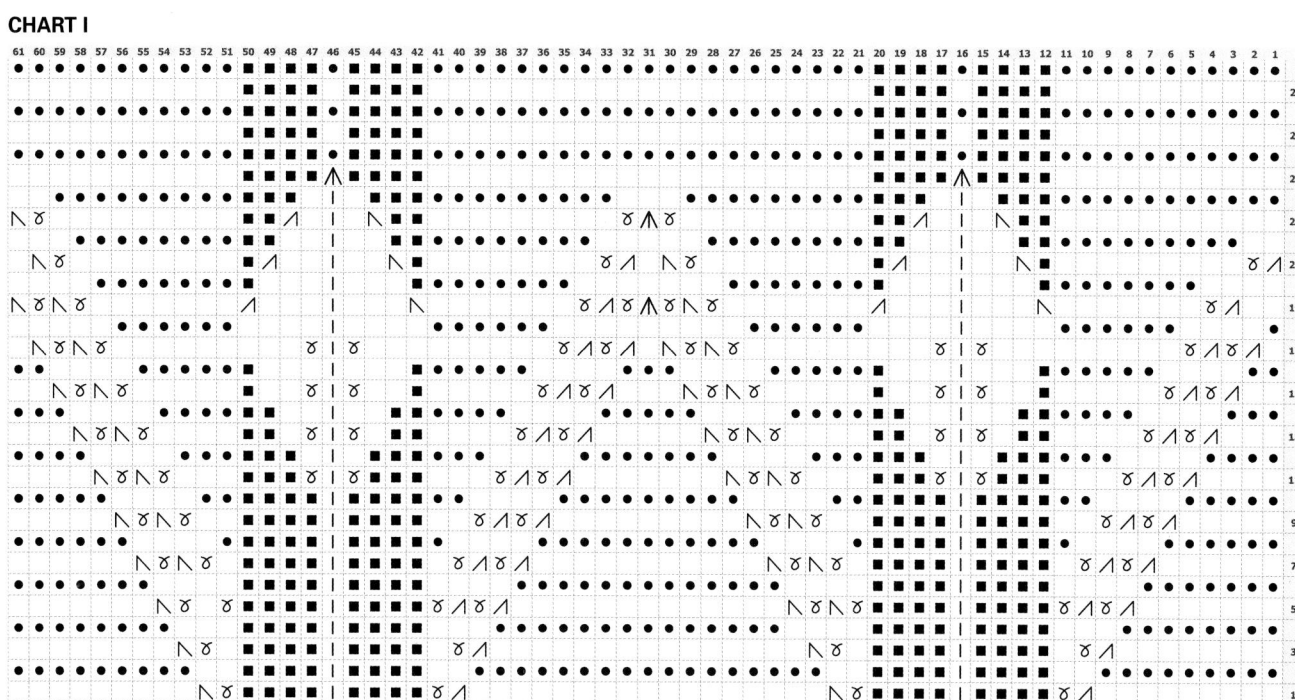

End with these 12 sts | 1 repeat | Begin with these 11 sts

CHART II

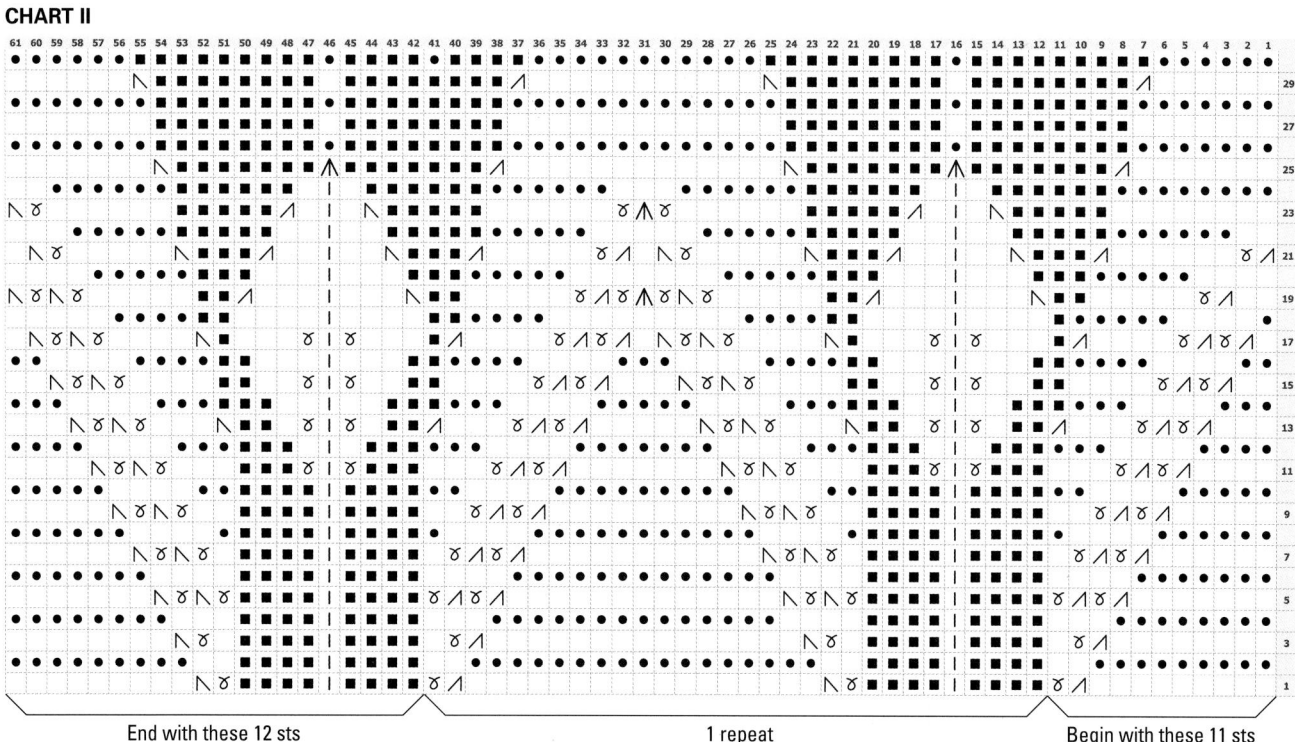

End with these 12 sts | 1 repeat | Begin with these 11 sts

FRENCH LILY

A slightly wide pullover with lily motifs in pink and violet tones, framed by rolled edges in two colors. The sweater has a round neck with two rolled edges.

SKILL LEVEL
Intermediate to Experienced

SIZES
S/M (L/XL)

FINISHED MEASUREMENTS
Chest: 51¼ (58¼) in / 130 (148) cm
Total Length: 28¼ (30) in / 72 (76) cm
Sleeve Length: 18¼ (19) in / 46 (48) cm, or desired length

MATERIALS
Yarn:
CYCA #3 (DK, light worsted) Rowan Felted Tweed (50% Merino wool, 25% alpaca, 25% viscose, 191 yd/175 m / 50 g)
Yarn Colors and Amounts:
Color 1: Camel 157: 200 (250) g
Color 2: Phantom 153: 100 (150) g
Color 3: Barn Red 196: 150 (200) g
Color 4: Frozen 185: 50 (50) g
Color 5: Clay 177: 100 (150) g
Color 6: Peony 183: 50 (100) g
Color 7: Amethyst 192: 50 (50) g
Color 8: Ancient 172: 50 (100) g
Needles: U. S. sizes 2.5 and 4 / 3 and 3.5 mm: circulars (2 x 32 in / 80 cm in larger size) and sets of 5 dpn.
If you work two-color stranded knitting more tightly than one-color knitting, use U. S. 6 / 4 mm for those sections.

GAUGE
22 sts in stockinette with U. S. 4 / 3.5 mm or pattern with U. S. 6 / 4 mm = 4 in / 10 cm.
Adjust needle size to obtain correct gauge if necessary.

BODY

The body is knitted in the round from the bottom up.

Rolled Edge 1: With smaller circular and Color 6, CO 286 (326) sts. Join, being careful not to twist cast-on row; pm for beginning of rnd. Knit 7 rnds and then set piece aside.

Rolled Edge 2: With smaller circular and color 8, CO 286 (326) sts. Join, being careful not to twist cast-on row; pm for beginning of rnd. Knit 11 rnds.

Joining: Place Rolled Edge 2 behind Rolled Edge 1. With Color 6, join the two edges by working k2tog (1 st from each edge) around = 286 (326) sts. Change to Color 1 and knit 1 rnd. Pm at each side = 143 (163) sts each for front and back. Change to larger circular (size needed to obtain gauge in two-color stranded knitting) and work around in pattern following chart. Begin at arrow for your size and work rep to side marker = front. Work the same way for back. Work Rows 1-54 of chart once and then rep Rows 55-66 of chart until body measures a total of 18¼ (19) in / 46 (48) cm.

Divide body at side markers and work back and front separately.

Back: Continue in pattern, working back and forth. When piece measures a total of 26½ (28) in / 67 (71) cm, BO from outer edge of shoulder on each side. On every other row, BO 8-8-8-8-8-9 (9-9-9-10-10-10) sts. *At the same time*, 1¼ in / 3 cm before full length, BO the center 41 (45) sts for back neck. Work each side separately.

Right side: At neck edge, on every other row, BO 1 st 2 times. No sts rem.

Left side: Work as for right side, reversing shaping to correspond.

Front: Work as for back until 3¼ in / 8 cm before full length. BO the center 31 (35) sts for front neck. Work each side separately.

Right side: At neck edge, on every other row, BO 2 sts 2 times and 1 st 3 times. Complete shoulder shaping. No sts rem.

Left side: Work as for right side, reversing shaping to correspond.

SLEEVES

The sleeves are worked in the round.

Rolled Edge 1: With smaller dpn and Color 6, CO 51 (55) sts. Divide sts onto dpn and join; pm for beginning of rnd. Knit 7 rnds and then set piece aside.

Rolled Edge 2: With smaller dpn and color 8, CO 51 (55) sts. Divide sts onto dpn and join; pm for beginning of rnd. Knit 11 rnds.

Joining: Place Rolled Edge 2 behind Rolled Edge 1. With Color 6, join the two edges by working k2tog (1 st from each edge) around = 51 (55) sts. Change to Color 1 and knit 1 rnd. Change to larger dpn (size needed to obtain gauge in two-color stranded knitting) and work around in pattern following chart. See arrow for center of sleeve and count back to determine starting point for your size. Begin knitting pattern on Row 55 of chart, and rep Rows 55-66 for whole sleeve. *At the same time*, on every 5th rnd, increase 2 sts centered on underarm until there are 89 (105) sts. Continue without further increases until sleeve is 18¼ (19) in / 46 (48) cm long. BO. Knit second sleeve the same way.

FINISHING

Seam shoulders.

Neckband: The neckband consists of two rolled edges.

Rolled Edge 1: With smaller circular and Color 6, pick up and knit 70 (73) sts across front neck and 57 (60) sts across back neck. Work 1 rnd of (k1tbl) around and then knit 7 rnds. BO.

Rolled Edge 2: With smaller circular and color 8, pick up and knit 70 (73) sts across front neck and 57 (60) sts across back of rolled edge. Work 1 rnd of (k1tbl) around and then knit 11 rnds. BO. Let edges roll forward. Attach sleeves.

Weave in all ends neatly on WS. Gently steam press on WS under damp pressing cloth.

CHART

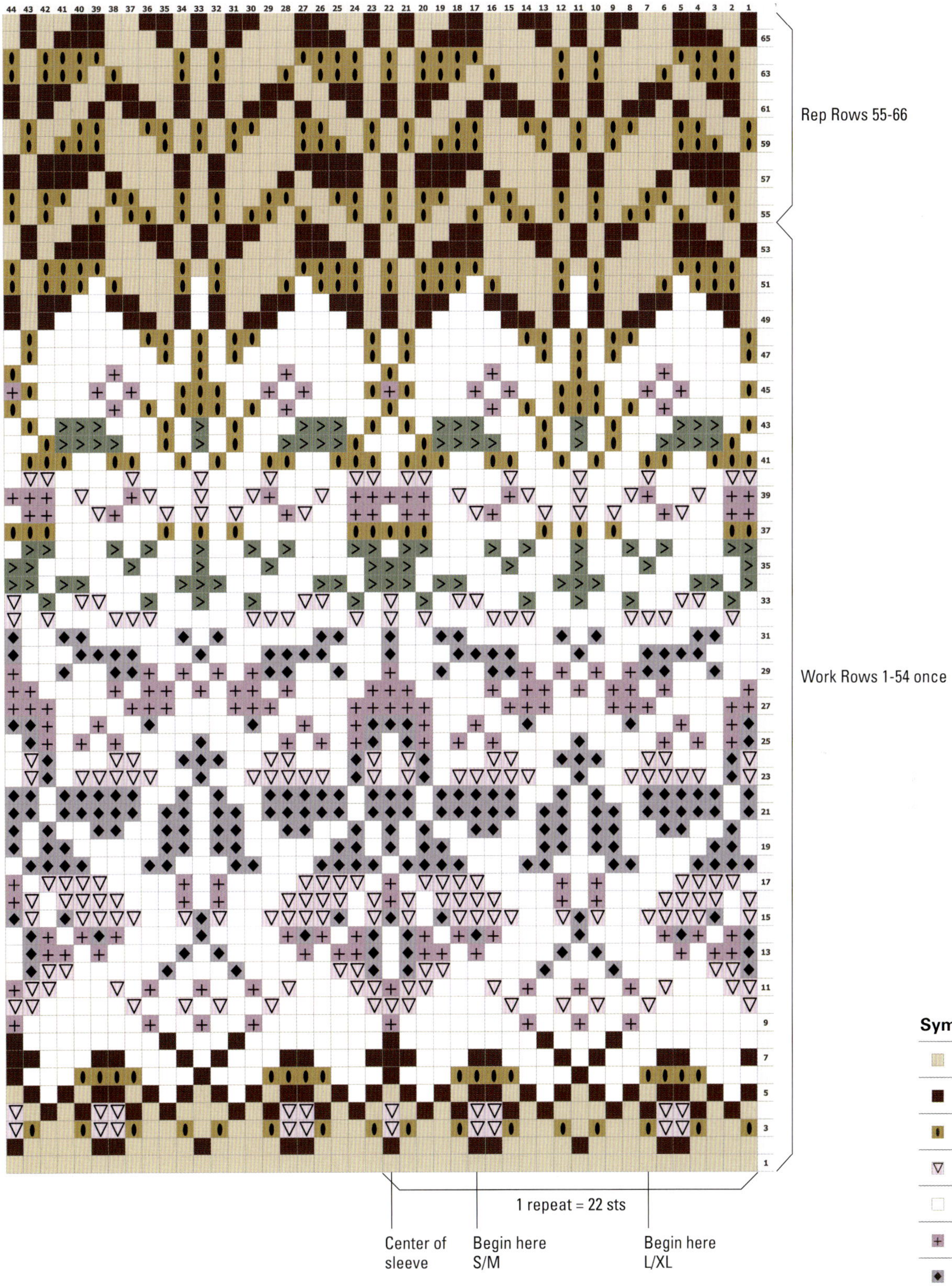

Rep Rows 55-66

Work Rows 1-54 once

1 repeat = 22 sts

Center of sleeve

Begin here S/M

Begin here L/XL

Symbols Key

▢	Color 1
■	Color 2
▮	Color 3
▽	Color 4
▢	Color 5
+	Color 6
◆	Color 7
▷	Color 8

HOPE

A lovely, charming cardigan with a shaped waist and edgings worked in slip stitch. I knitted two rolled edges around the neckline. The front bands are crocheted, too, so there are many exciting techniques in the same garment.

SKILL LEVEL
Intermediate to Experienced

SIZES
S (M, L, XL, XXL)

FINISHED MEASUREMENTS
Chest: 34¼ (36¾, 39½, 43¼, 47¼) in / 87 (93, 100, 110, 120) cm
Total Length: 22¾ (23¾, 24½, 25¼, 26) in / 58 (60, 62, 64, 66) cm
Sleeve Length: 19¼ (19¾, 19¾, 20, 20) in / 49 (50, 50, 51, 51) cm

MATERIALS
Yarn:
CYCA #2 (sport, baby) Hillesvåg Ask/Hifa 2 (100% Norwegian wool, 344 yd/315 m / 100 g)

Yarn Colors and Amounts:
Color 1: Light Gray Heather 6054: 250 (250, 300, 300, 350) g
Color 2: Light Blue-Purple 6041: 100 (100, 200, 200, 200) g
Color 3: Light Blue-Violet Heather 6541: 50 (100, 100, 150, 150) g
Color 4: Brown Heather 6102: 50 (50, 100, 100, 100) g
Needles: U. S. sizes 1.5 and 2.5 / 2.5 and 3 mm circulars and sets of 5 dpn.
If you work two-color stranded knitting more tightly than one-color knitting, use U. S. 4 / 3.5 mm for those sections.
Crochet Hook: U. S. B-1 or C-2 / 2.5 mm
Notions: 9 buttons to match colors in cardigan. Approx. 1.09 yd / 1 m of ribbon to cover cut edges of steek.

GAUGE
24 sts in stockinette/pattern with U. S. 2.5 / 3 mm or pattern with U. S. 4 / 3.5 mm = 4 in / 10 cm.
Adjust needle size to obtain correct gauge if necessary.

NOTE: Read through the pattern fully before you begin to knit. There are several places where some steps occur simultaneously. Mark each occurrence of "*at the same time*" so you will be aware of these simultaneous steps.

BODY

With smaller circular and Color 3, CO 209 (225, 241, 265, 289) sts + 6 sts at center front for steek.

Steek: Purl steek sts; do not include steek sts in stitch counts. To make cutting and sewing later easier, and to secure the yarns, work the 2 center sts with pattern color.

Knit 1 row on WS. Turn and join to work in the round. Knit 1 rnd, purl 1 rnd. Work pattern following Chart I, 1 repeat in length. Pm as follows: 6 steek sts = center front, pm, count 52 (56, 60, 66, 72) sts, pm = right front. Count 105 (113, 121, 133, 145) = back, pm, count 52 (56, 60, 66, 72) st = left front. Change to Color 1 and larger circular. Knit 1 rnd, purl 1 rnd and then knit around in stockinette for 2¾ (2¾, 3½, 4, 4¼) in / 7 (7, 9, 10, 11) cm. Now work pattern following Chart II, beginning at arrow and continuing around. Work Rnds 1-32 of chart and then rep Rnds 33-50.

Shape Sides: *At the same time*, when body measures a total of 3¼ (3¼, 4, 4¼, 4¾) in / 8 (8, 10, 11, 12) cm, decrease at each side on every 4th rnd 8 times as follows: Knit until 2 sts rem on right front, k2tog tbl, on back, k2tog, knit until 2 sts rem on back, k2tog tbl, k2tog on left front = 177 (193, 209, 233, 257) + 6 steek sts. Continue knitting straight up until body measures 7½ (8, 8¼, 8¾, 9) in / 19 (20, 21, 22, 23) cm. Now increase at each side of each marker on every 4th rnd 7 times = 205 (221, 237, 261, 285) sts + 6 steek sts. Continue straight up until body measures a total of 14½ (15, 15½, 15¾, 16¼) in / 37 (38, 39, 40, 41) cm.

Shape Armholes: Knit until 5 sts rem before side marker, BO 10 sts, knit until 5 sts before next side marker, BO 10 sts. On next rnd, CO 6 sts at each side over bound-off sts = steeks. Purl steek sts; do not include in stitch counts. Continue knitting in the round.

At each side of back and front (on each side of side steeks) on every other rnd: decrease 2 sts 2 times and 1 st 4 times. Continue without further shaping to Row 40 of Chart II. Now work in pattern following Chart III; work Rows 1-8 once, then rep Rows 9-18 for rest of body—see arrow for where to begin right front, and make sure Chart III pattern follows Chart II pattern naturally.

Neckline: *At the same time*, 4¾ in / 12 cm before total length, BO for front neck and work back and forth: BO the 6 front steek sts and BO 10 sts on each side of steek. Then, on every other row, at neck edge: decrease 1 st 9 (9, 10, 10, 10) times. Continue in pattern until body measures 22¾ (23¾, 24½, 25¼, 26) in / 58 (60, 62, 64, 66) cm. BO all sts.

SLEEVES

With smaller dpn and Color 1, CO 72 (74, 76, 78, 80) sts. Knit 1 row on WS; turn. Divide sts onto 4 dpn and join. Knit 1 rnd, purl 1 rnd. Work around in pattern following Chart I, 3 rep in length. *At the same time*, decrease 2 sts centered on underarm on every 3rd rnd 8 times = 56 (58, 60, 62, 64) sts. After completing chart 1 pattern, change to Color 1 and larger dpn. Knit 1 rnd, purl 1 rnd. Knit rest of sleeve in stockinette. Knit straight up for 1½ in / 4 cm.

Increases on Sleeve: On every 5th rnd, increase 2 sts centered on underarm until there are 78 (84, 88, 92, 98) sts. Continue straight up until sleeve is 19¼ (19¾, 19¾, 20, 20) in / 49 (50, 50, 51, 51) cm long.

Sleeve Cap: BO 5 sts knit until 5 sts rem, BO 5 sts. Continue, working back and forth. On every other row, at each side of sleeve, BO 1 st 9 (9, 10, 10, 10) times. On every 4th row, BO 1 st 5 (5, 6, 6, 6) times, BO 4 sts at beginning of next 8 (8, 8, 10, 10) rows. BO rem sts. Make second sleeve the same way.

Facing: With WS facing, using smaller needles and Color 1, pick up and knit approx. 134 (140, 148, 162, 172) sts around sleeve cap. Work 1 rnd k1tbl and then knit 6 rnds. BO. Work facing the same way on second sleeve.

FINISHING

Weave in all ends neatly on WS. *Gently* steam press on WS under a damp pressing cloth. Machine-stitch zigzag line on each side of center steek sts on front and armholes. Carefully cut steeks open up center. Join shoulders.

Neckband: The neckband consists of two rolled edges.

Rolled Edge 1: With smaller circular and Color 1, pick up and knit 45 (46, 47, 48, 49) sts across right front neck, 38 (40, 42, 44, 46) sts on back neck, and 45 (46, 47, 48, 49) sts across left front neck Work 1 row of (k1tbl) across and then work 13 rows in stockinette. Knit 1 row on WS and BO. *At the same time*, decrease at shoulders and 1 st at beginning and end of neck edge, on every other

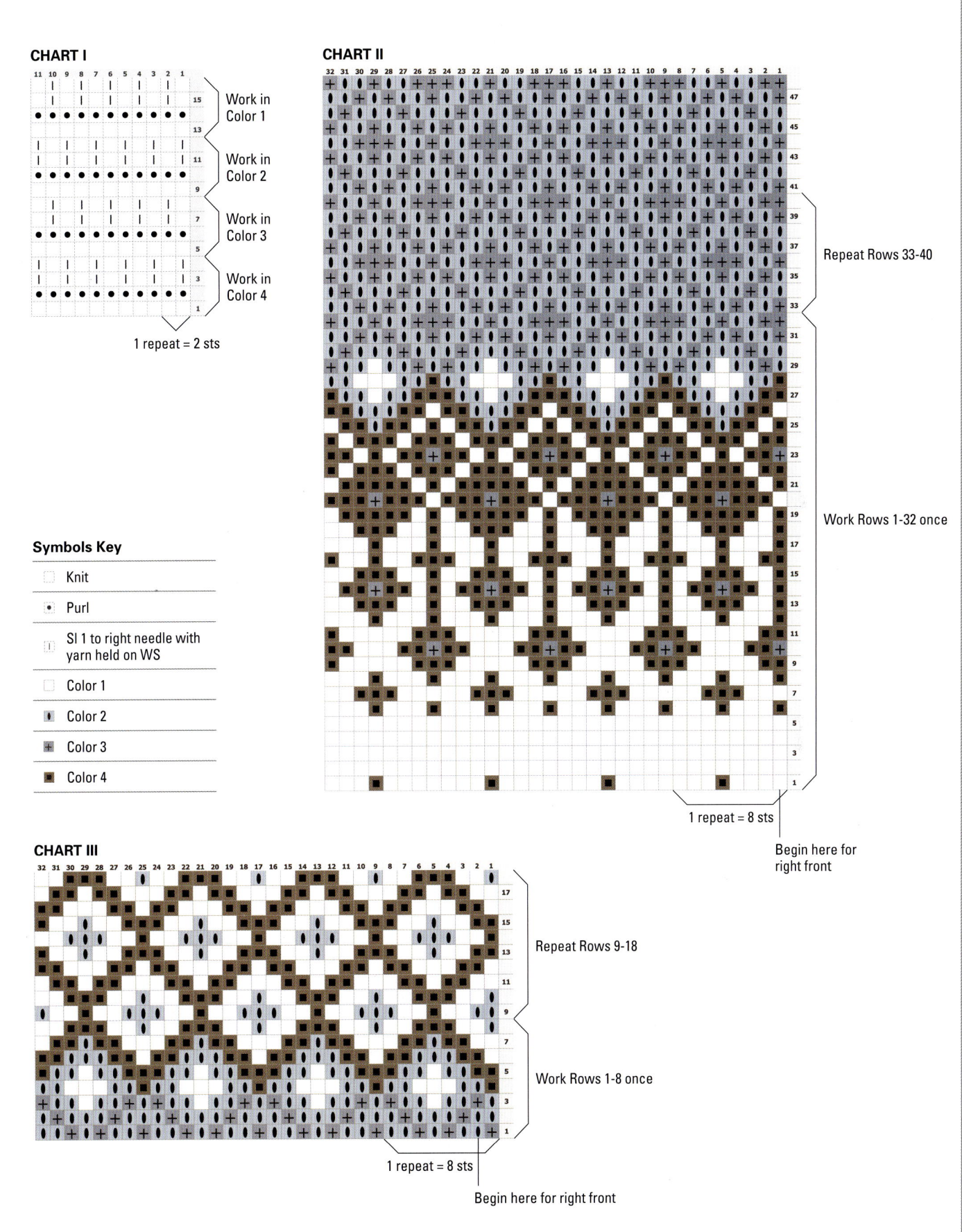

row (on RS): pm at neck edge over each shoulder seam, K1, k2tog tbl, knit until 2 sts rem before marker on right shoulder, k2tog tbl, k2tog, knit until 2 sts before next marker and k2tog tbl, k2tog, knit until 3 sts rem on row and k2tog, k1.

Rolled Edge 2: With smaller circular and Color 3, pick up and knit sts on underside of rolled edge 1 (towards body), 1 st in each st. Work as for first rolled edge, but work 15 rows in stockinette, knit 1 row on WS, and then BO.

Crochet Tip: Work 1 sc in each of next 5 sts, skip 1 st to keep the edging the right tension.

Left Front Band: With crochet hook and Color 1, work 1 row sc along left front edge; turn and work 1 row sc back. Change to Color 2 and work 2 rows sc. Change to Color 3 and work 2 rows sc + 1 row with crab st (= sc worked from left to right). Cut yarn and fasten off.

Right Front Band: Mark placement of 9 buttons on left band. I grouped the buttons in threes with the bottom button 1¼ in / 3 cm from lower edge. I spaced the buttonholes 2½ in / 6 cm apart. The top one is ⅜ in / 1 cm below top edge.

Work right band as for left band, but on Row 3, make the buttonholes: ch 4, skip 3 sc, and work 1 sc in next sc. On next row, work 3 sc around each ch-4 loop.

Sew on buttons, spaced to match buttonholes.

Attach sleeves and fold facings over cut edges. Sew down smoothly on WS. Sew a ribbon on back of each front band to cover cut steek edges. *Gently* steam press on WS under a damp pressing cloth. Let rolled edges roll smoothly at neck.

OASIS

Oasis was part of a series of designs inspired by Dutch porcelain. I created a good contrast with a mixture of single-color yarn and a lightly heathered tweed yarn. The jacket has a fine fit with set-in sleeves, and it's closed with clasps.

SKILL LEVEL
Intermediate to Experienced

SIZES
XS (S, M, L, XL XXL)

FINISHED MEASUREMENTS
Chest: 30¾ (34¾, 37¾, 41¼, 43¼, 50) in / 78 (88, 96, 105, 110, 127) cm
Total Length: 19¾ (22, 22½, 22¾, 25¼, 26) in / 50 (56, 57, 58, 64, 66) cm
Sleeve Length: 17¼ (19, 19, 19¼, 19¾, 19¾) in / 44 (48, 48, 49, 50, 50) cm

MATERIALS
Yarn:
CYCA #3 (DK, light worsted) Du Store Alpakka Sterk (40% Merino wool, 40% alpaca, 20% polyamide, 150 yd/137 m / 50 g)
and
CYCA #3 (DK, light worsted) Rowan Felted Tweed (50% Merino wool, 25% alpaca, 25% viscose, 191 yd/175 m / 50 g)
Yarn Colors and Amounts:
Color 1: Sterk Medium Gray 822: 200 (250, 250, 300, 300, 350) g
Color 2: Sterk White 851: 50 (50, 50, 100, 100, 100) g
Color 3: Felted Tweed Seafarer 170: 200 (200, 250, 250, 300, 350) g
Color 4: Felted Tweed Peony 183: 50 (50, 50, 50, 100, 100) g

Needles: U. S. sizes 2.5 and 4 / 3 and 3.5 mm: circulars and sets of 5 dpn.
If you work two-color stranded knitting more tightly than one-color knitting, use U. S. 6 / 4 mm for those sections.
Notions: 3 clasps. Approx. 1.3 yd / 1.2 m ribbon to cover cut edges of front steek.

GAUGE
22 sts and 24 rnds in stockinette/pattern with U. S. 4 / 3.5 mm or U. S. 6 / 4 mm = 4 x 4 in / 10 x 10 cm.
Adjust needle size to obtain correct gauge if necessary.

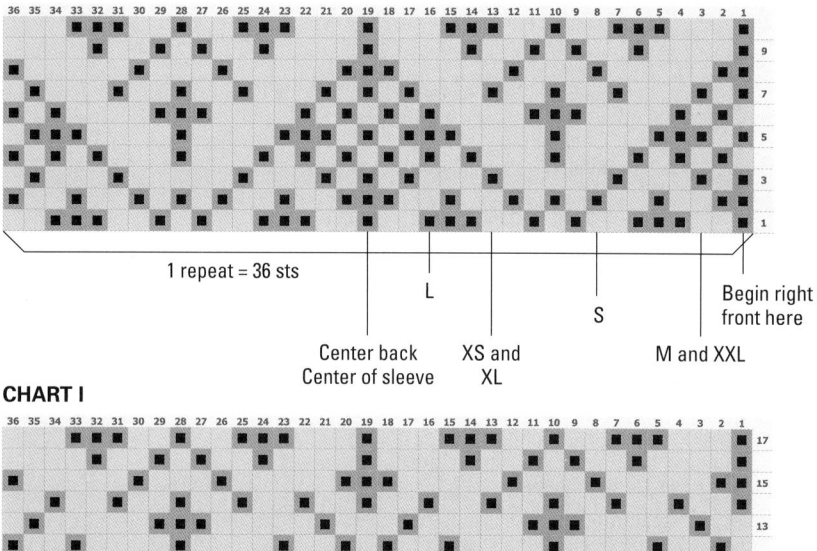

CHART I — 1 repeat = 36 sts
Center back / Center of sleeve · XS and XL · S · M and XXL · Begin right front here · L

CHART I — 1 repeat = 36 sts
Center back / Center of sleeve · Begin right front here

NOTE: Read through the pattern fully before you begin to knit. There are several places where some steps occur simultaneously. Mark each occurrence of "*at the same time*" so you will be aware of these simultaneous steps.

BODY

The body is knitted in the round from the bottom up.
With smaller circular and Color 4, CO 169 (191, 213, 231, 241, 281) sts + 7 sts for steek
Steek: Do not include steek sts in stitch counts. Always work the 7 steek sts in purl with color most used in pattern. To make cutting and sewing later easier, and to secure the yarns, work the center st with pattern color.

Join, being careful not to twist cast-on row; pm for beginning of rnd. Knit 7 rnds in stockinette, purl 3 rnds, knit 1 rnd = rolled edge. Pm at sides of work with 42 (48, 54, 58, 60, 70) sts for each side of front and 85 (95, 105, 115, 121, 141) sts for back. Change to larger circular (size needed to obtain gauge in two-color stranded knitting). Work in pattern following Chart I. Begin at arrow for right front and work in pattern to side marker. Begin at arrow for your size on back and work to next side marker. Work left front to mirror-image right front. Work 1 rep of chart in length. Now work in pattern following Chart II, making sure pattern naturally follows from Chart I pattern.

Continue until body measures approx. 11 (12¾, 12¼, 11¾, 14½, 14½) in / 28 (32, 31, 30, 37, 37) cm from rolled edge.
Shape Armholes on Each Side: Knit until 4 (4, 4, 4, 5, 5) sts before first marker, BO 8 (8, 8, 8, 10, 10) sts, knit until 4 (4, 4, 4, 5, 5) sts rem before next marker, BO 8 (8, 8, 8, 10, 10) sts, and knit to end of rnd. On next rnd, CO 5 new sts over gap at each side for armhole steeks. Always purl steek sts.
Decrease for Armholes: On each side of each armhole steek, on every other rnd, decrease 1 st 3 times, and then on every 4th rnd, decrease 1 st 2 (2, 2, 3, 4, 4) times.
At the same time, after working 4 (5, 5, 5, 6, 6) rep in length from Chart II, work in pattern following Chart III, 1 rep in length, making sure pattern naturally follows from Chart II pattern. When pattern is complete, work rem length with Color 2.
Shape Neck: When 3¼ in / 8 cm from total length, BO the center front 22 (26, 30, 26, 26, 26) sts + the 7 steek sts for front neck = 11 (13, 15, 13, 13, 13) sts on each side of steek. Work back and forth in pattern. On each side of neck, on every other row, BO 2 sts once and 1 st 4 (4, 4, 5, 5, 5) times.
Back: When 1¼ in / 3 cm from total length, divide body at sides. BO the 5 steek sts at each side and work each side of back separately.
Neck and Shoulder Shaping: BO the center 31 (33, 35, 35, 37, 37) sts on back. Work each side separately. Continue decreasing at neck edge on every other row: 1 st 2 times. *At the same time*, shape shoulder by binding off on every other row: 5-5-6 (6-7-7, 8-8-8, 9-9-10, 9-9-10, 12-13-13) sts. No more sts rem on shoulder. Work

Symbols Key

- ▨ Color 1
- ☐ Color 2
- ▣ Color 3
- ▥ Color 4

CHART III

1 repeat = 36 sts · Center back · Begin right front here

opposite side to correspond.
Front: Shape shoulders as for back. BO rem sts.

SLEEVES

With smaller dpn and Color 4, CO 45 (47, 49, 51, 53, 57) sts. Divide sts onto dpn and join. Knit 7 rnds in stockinette, purl 3 rnds, knit 1 rnd = rolled edge. Change to larger dpn (size needed to obtain gauge in two-color stranded knitting). Work in pattern following Chart I for 1 rep in length. See arrow for center of sleeve and count back to determine first st of rnd for your size. Next, work in pattern following Chart II, making sure pattern naturally follows from Chart I pattern. *At the same time*, increase 2 sts centered on underarm on every 6th rnd (increases begin on 6th rnd after rolled edge) until there are 77 (83, 87, 93, 99, 105) sts. When sleeve measures a total of 17¼ (19, 19, 19¼, 19¾, 19¾) in / 44 (48, 48, 49, 50, 50) cm, divide sleeve in two at underarm. Continue in pattern, working back and forth.
Sleeve Cap: At each side, BO 4 (4, 4, 4, 5, 5) sts and then, on every other row: BO 2 sts once, and 1 st 4 (5, 5, 5, 5, 6) times. On every 4th row: BO 1 st 2 times. BO 4 sts at beginning of next 6 (8, 8, 8, 10, 10) rows. BO rem sts.
Sleeve Facing: With WS facing, smaller needles, and Color 3, pick up and knit approx. 116 (122, 134, 142, 150, 158) sts around top of sleeve. Work 1 row k1tbl and then work 5 rows back and forth in stockinette. BO. Make second sleeve the same way.

FINISHING

Weave in all ends neatly on WS. *Gently* steam press all pieces on WS under a damp pressing cloth. Machine-stitch zigzag line on each side of center steek sts on front and armholes. Carefully cut steeks open up center. Join shoulders.
Front Bands: With smaller circular and Color 4, with RS facing, pick up and knit approx. 101 (115, 121, 123, 134, 136) sts along left front. Work 1 row k1tbl on WS. Purl 1 row, knit 1 row, and then work 6 rows in stockinette. BO. Work a corresponding edging on right front.
Neckband: With smaller circular and Color 4, with RS facing, pick up and knit 32 (34, 35, 36, 37, 38) sts along bound-off sts of right front, 42 (44, 46, 48, 50, 52) sts along back neck, and 32 (34, 35, 36, 37, 38) sts along bound-off sts of left front. Purl 1 row, knit 1 row, work 8 rows in stockinette. BO.
Sew 3 clasps on front of jacket and sew ribbon on back of front bands to cover cut edges of steek.
Attach sleeves and fold facing over cut edges of steek; sew down facing.

BUTTERFLY
IN WINTERLAND

This gorgeous jacket is named after a song by Halvdan Sivertsen. It has a two-color pattern with butterflies and blocks, which requires concentration to knit. Block patterns in delicate colors along the edges frame the jacket.

SKILL LEVEL
Experienced

SIZES
S (M, L, XL, XXL)

FINISHED MEASUREMENTS
Chest: 34¾ (37, 40¼, 44, 48¾) in / 88 (94, 102, 112, 124) cm
Total Length: 22¾ (23¾, 24½, 25¼, 26) in / 58 (60, 62, 64, 66) cm
Sleeve Length: 19 (19¼, 19¼, 19¾, 19¾) in / 48 (49, 49, 50, 50) cm

MATERIALS
Yarn:
CYCA #2 (sport, baby) Hillesvåg Ask/Hifa 2 (100% Norwegian wool, 344 yd/315 m / 100 g)
Yarn Colors and Amounts:
Color 1: Light Gray 6054: 250 (250, 300, 300, 350) g
Color 2: Light Blue-Violet 6541: 150 (200, 200, 250, 250) g
Color 3: Purple 6077: 50 (50, 50, 50, 50) g
Color 4: Bright Apple Green Heather 6588: 50 (100, 100, 100, 100) g
Needles: U. S. sizes 1.5 and 2.5 / 2.5 and 3 mm circulars and sets of 5 dpn.
If you work two-color stranded knitting more tightly than one-color knitting, use U. S. 4 / 3.5 mm for those sections.
Crochet Hook: U. S. B-1 or C-2 / 2.5 mm
Notions: 10 buttons to match colors in cardigan. Approx. 1.4 yd / 1.3 m ribbon to cover cut edges of steek.

GAUGE
24 sts in stockinette pattern with U. S. 2.5 / 3 mm or pattern with U. S. 4 / 3.5 mm = 4 in / 10 cm.
Adjust needle size to obtain correct gauge if necessary.

NOTE: Read through the pattern fully before you begin to knit. There are several places where some steps occur simultaneously. Mark each occurrence of "*at the same time*" so you will be aware of these simultaneous steps.

BODY

The body is knitted in the round from the bottom up.
With smaller circular and Color 4, CO 208 (224, 244, 268, 296) sts + 6 sts at center front for steek. Join, being careful not to twist cast-on row; pm for beginning of rnd.
Steek: Purl steek sts; do not include steek sts in stitch counts. To make cutting and sewing later easier, and to secure the yarns, work the 2 center sts with pattern color.
Knit 6 rnds in stockinette, purl 1 rnd = rolled edge. Work in pattern following Chart I for 1 rep of chart in length. On last rnd, CO 1 st at end of rnd = 209 (225, 245, 269, 297) sts. Pm as follows: 52 (56, 61, 67, 74) sts for right front, 105 (113, 123, 135, 149) sts for back, and 52 (56, 61, 67, 74) sts for left front. Make sure the 6 steek sts are centered between the two front pieces.
Change to larger circular (size needed to obtain gauge in two-color stranded knitting).
Begin at arrow for right front and work in pattern to side marker. Begin at arrow for your size on back and work in pattern across back. Work left front to mirror-image right front.
Front pieces: Work Rows 1-68 of chart and then rep Rows 69-76 for rest of work.
Back: Work Rows 1-84 on chart and then rep Rows 77-84 for rest of work.
When body measures approx. 14½ (15, 15½, 15¾, 15¾) in / 37 (38, 39, 40, 40) cm from rolled edge, BO 8 sts on each side for armholes: Knit until 4 sts before side marker, BO 8 sts, knit until 4 sts before next side marker, BO 8 sts. Knit to end of rnd. Set body aside.

SLEEVES

The sleeves are worked in the round. With smaller dpn and Color 4, CO 48 (48, 52, 52, 56) sts. Divide sts onto dpn and join. Knit 6 rnds in stockinette, purl 1 rnd = rolled edge. On last rnd, increase 1 (3, 1, 3, 3) sts evenly spaced around = 49 (51, 53, 55, 59) sts.
Pattern on Sleeves: Work in pattern following Chart I. Work Rows 1-8 of chart and then Rows 3-9. Change to larger dpn (size needed to obtain gauge in two-color stranded knitting). Work in charted pattern for back. See arrow for center of sleeve and count back to determine first st of rnd for your size. Work Rows 1-84 of chart once and then rep Rows 77-84 for rest of sleeve.
Shape Sleeve: *At the same time*, after completing Chart I, increase 2 sts centered on underarm on every 5th rnd until there are 93 (97, 101, 111, 119) sts.
When sleeve measures a total of 19 (19¼, 19¼, 19¾, 19¾) in / 48 (49, 49, 50, 50) cm, make sure you are on same rnd in pattern as on back. BO 4 sts, knit until 4 sts rem and BO last 4 sts. Set sleeve aside while you knit second sleeve the same way.

JOINING BODY AND SLEEVES

Place all pieces on larger circular: right front, right sleeve, back, left sleeve, left front and steek = 363 (387, 415, 459, 503) sts total + 6 steek sts. Pm at each intersection of body and sleeve = 4 markers. Continuing in pattern, on 2nd rnd, begin decreasing for raglan:
Raglan Shaping: Knit until 2 sts before first marker, k2tog tbl, sl m, k2tog. Decrease the same way at each marker. Decrease the same way on every rnd 5 (6, 6, 8, 9) times = 323 (339, 367, 395, 431) sts rem. Now decrease as est on every other rnd a total of 25 (26, 27, 30, 34) times, and then on every rnd 3 times.
Neck Shaping: *At the same time*, when 6 raglan decrease rnds rem, BO the center 26 (28, 30, 32, 32) sts on front + the 6 steek sts = 13 (14, 15, 16, 16) sts on each side of steek. Work back and forth. On each side of neck on every other row, BO 2 sts once and 1 st 2 (2, 3, 3, 4) times. Continue with raglan shaping until all decreases have been worked. BO rem sts.

FINISHING

Weave in all ends neatly on WS. *Gently* steam press all pieces on WS under a damp pressing cloth. Machine-stitch 1 zigzag and 1 straight line on each side of center steek sts on front. Carefully cut steeks open up center. Seam underarms.
Front Bands, Left Front: With crochet hook and Color 4, work 1 row sc along left front edge; turn and work 1 row sc back; turn and work 1 more row sc. Change to Color 3 and work 2 rows sc. Change to Color 1 and work 1 row sc. Change to Color 4 and work 2 rows sc. Cut yarn and fasten off.
Right Front Band: Mark placement of 10 buttons on left band, with top one ¼ in / 0.5 cm from top edge and lowest ¼ in / 0.5 cm from lower

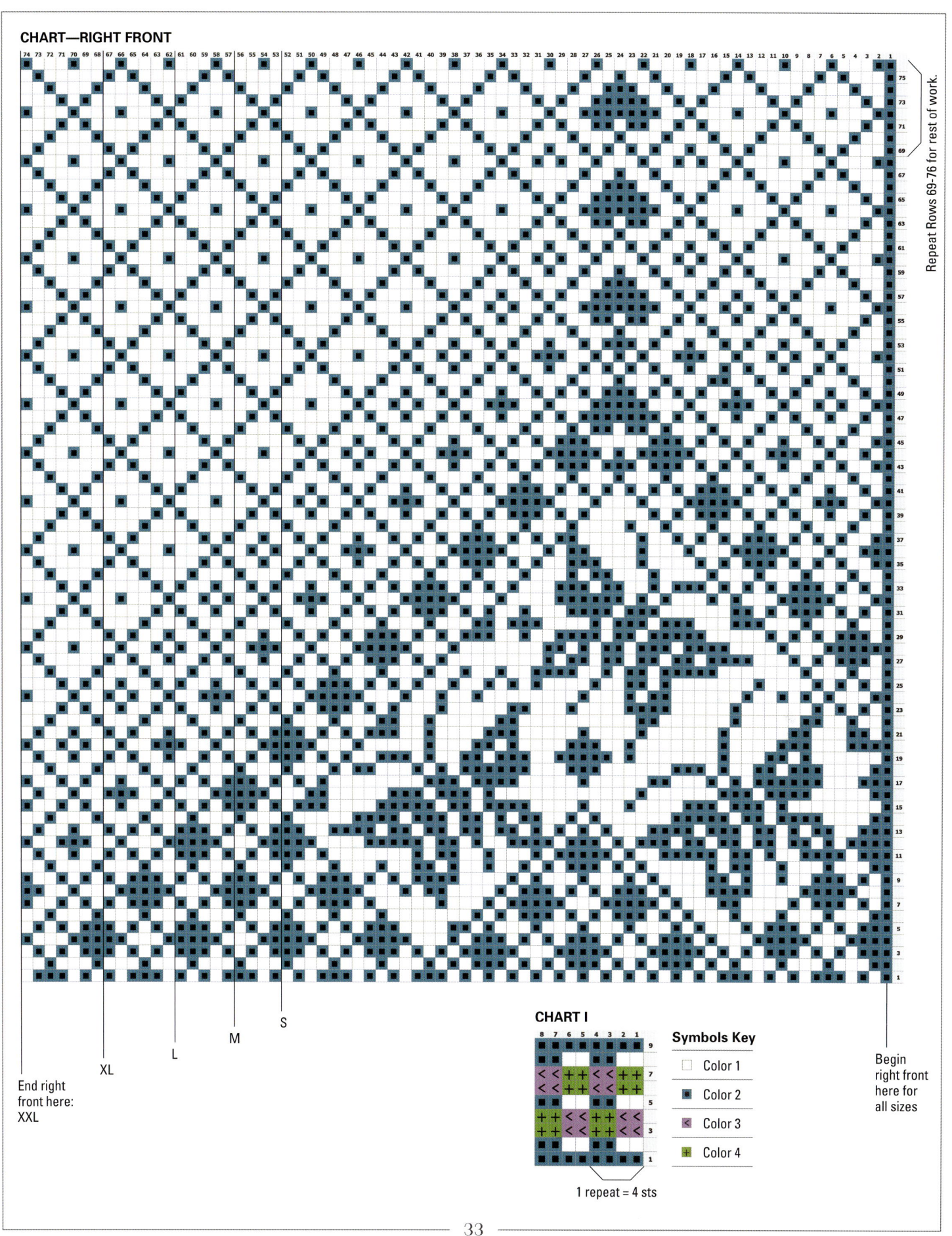

edge. Crochet edging as for left band, but on Row 3, make each buttonhole as follows: Ch 3, skip 3 sc and work 1 sc in next sc. On next row, work 3 sc around each ch-3 loop.

Neckband: With smaller circular and Color 2, with RS facing, pick up and knit 124 (128, 132, 136, 140) sts around neck and top of front bands. Begin by picking up at fold of right band and finish at fold of left band. On WS, work 1 row k1tbl. Work in pattern following Chart I for 1 rep in length. Change to Color 4 and knit 2 rows. On last row (on WS), decrease 10 sts evenly spaced across. Work 14 rows stockinette and BO. Fold edge double to WS and sew down smoothly. Sew buttons on left band matching buttonholes. Gently steam press jacket on WS under damp pressing cloth. Sew a ribbon on back of front bands to cover cut steek edges.

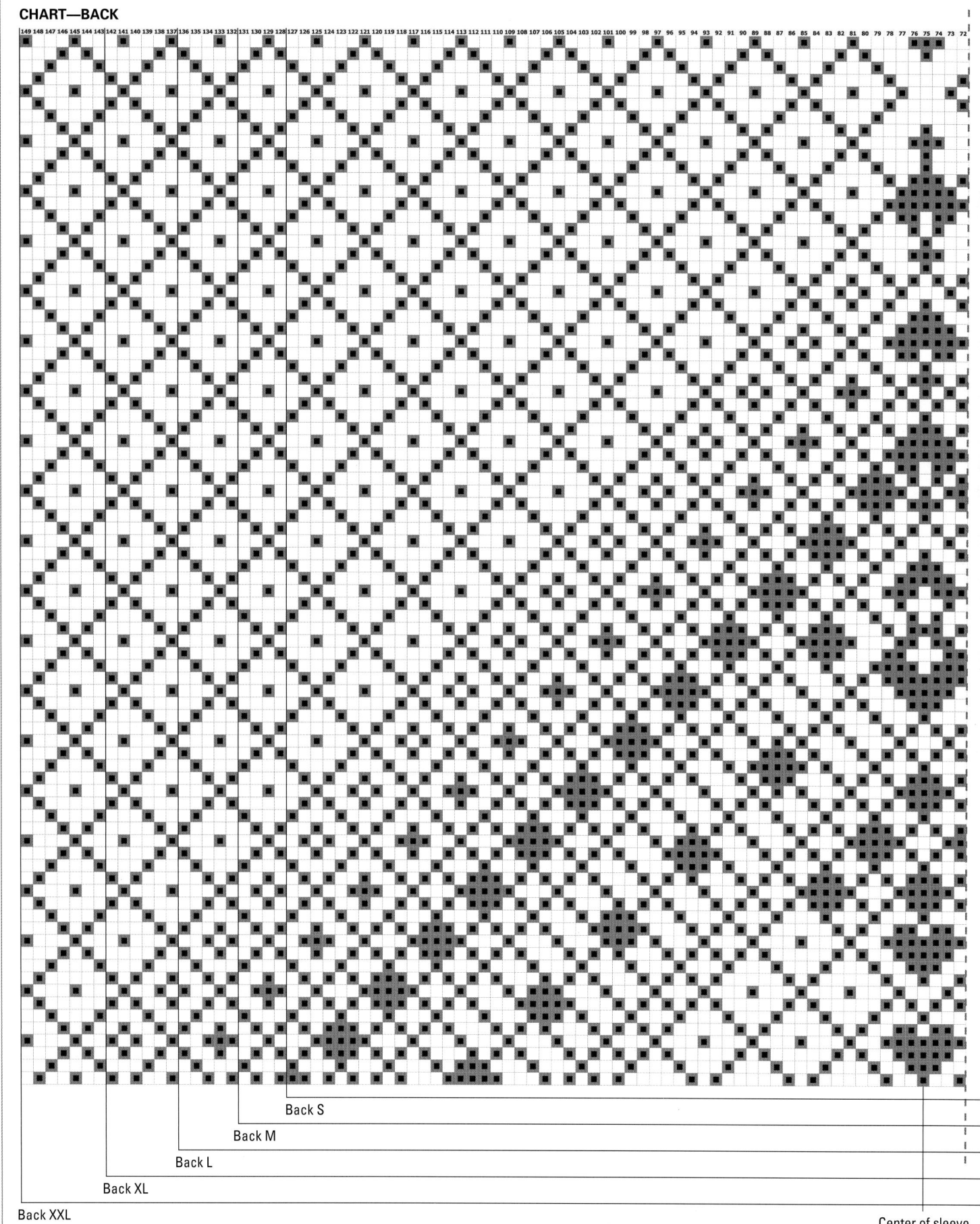

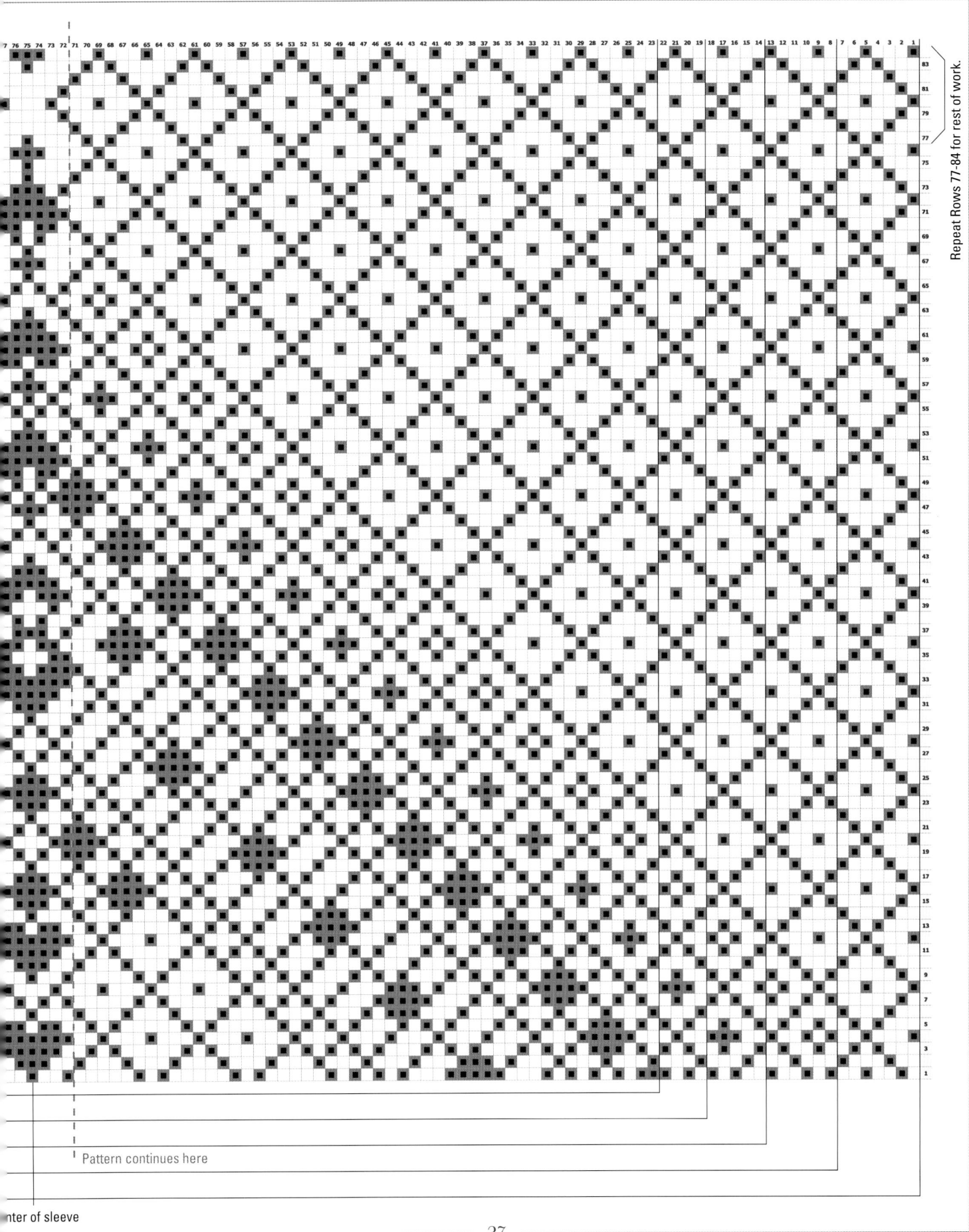

MYRA

You'll love this super easy, soft cardigan, with set-in sleeves. The lovely wave pattern on the lower edges of the body and sleeves is reminiscent of Viking ships on a sea expedition. For a pullover with the same pattern, see Tumi on page 88.

SKILL LEVEL
Intermediate

SIZES
S (M, L, XL, XXL)

FINISHED MEASUREMENTS
Chest: 35½ (38½, 41¼, 44, 50) in / 90 (98, 105, 112, 127) cm
Total Length: 24 (24¾, 25½, 26½, 27¼) in / 61 (63, 65, 67, 69) cm
Sleeve Length: 18½ (19, 19, 19¼, 19¼) in / 47 (48, 48, 49, 49) cm

MATERIALS
Yarn:
CYCA #1 (light fingering) Naturally Yarns New Zealand Amuri 4-ply (75% Merino wool, 25% possum, 262 yd/240 m / 50 g)
Yarn Colors and Amounts:
Lilac Heather 4036: 200 (250, 250, 300, 300) g
Needles: U. S. sizes 1.5 and 4 / 2.5 and 3.5 mm: circulars and sets of 5 dpn
Notions: 6 buttons in color to match sweater

GAUGE
24 sts in ribbing with larger needles = 4 in / 10 cm.
Adjust needle size to obtain correct gauge if necessary.

BODY

The body is worked back and forth from the bottom up.

With larger circular, CO 217 (235, 253, 271, 307) sts. Knit 4 rows back and forth. Work pattern following the chart: Begin with first 18 sts on chart, work 18-st repeat 11 (12, 13, 14, 16) times, and end with last st on chart. Work 1 rep in length.

Dividing for Front and Back: Count 54 (58, 63, 67, 76) sts and pm = right front. Count 109 (119, 127, 137, 155) sts and pm = back. The rem 54 (58, 63, 67, 76) sts = left front. Continue, repeating Rows 43-44 of chart for reminder of piece, until body measures 14½ (15, 15½, 15½, 15¾) in / 37 (38, 39, 39, 40) cm.

Right Front: Now work only over the 54 (58, 63, 67, 76) sts of right front. Begin shaping armhole and V-neck *at the same time*:

Shape Armhole: BO 5 sts on left side of front. Then, on every other row, BO 2 sts once, and 1 st 4 (4, 5, 5, 5) times; on every 4th row, BO 1 st 3 times.

V-Neck: Decrease 1 st on right side of front on every 3rd row 24 (25, 26, 27, 28) times.

Continue as est until front measures 8¼ (8¾, 9, 10, 10¾) in / 21 (22, 23, 25, 27) cm from first bound-off row of armhole. Now shape shoulder by binding off, from outer edge of shoulder: on every other row, BO 5-5-6 (6-6-7, 7-7-8, 8-8-9, 11-11-11) sts. No sts rem at shoulder.

Left Front: Work as for right front, reversing shaping to correspond.

Back: Shape armholes as for fronts and then continue straight up until back measures 8¼ (8¾, 9, 9¾, 10¾) in / 21 (22, 23, 25, 27) cm from first bound-off row of armhole.

Now shape back neck and shoulders *at the same time*.

Back Neck: BO the center 41 (45, 45, 49, 51) sts for back neck. Work each side separately and BO at neck edge on every other row: 2 sts 2 times.

Shape shoulders as for front. No sts rem at shoulder. Work opposite side to correspond.

SLEEVES

The sleeves are worked in the round. With larger dpn, CO 55 (55, 55, 55, 73) sts. Divide st onto dpn and join.

Knit 1 rnd, purl 1 rnd, knit 1 rnd, purl 1 rnd. Work pattern following the chart: Begin with first 18 sts on chart, work 18-st repeat 2 (2, 2, 2, 3) times and end with last st on chart. Work Rows 15-44 of chart and then rep Rows 43-44 for rest of sleeve.

Shape Sleeve: Increase 2 sts centered on underarm every 8th rnd until there are 87 (91, 97, 103, 111) sts. Continue without further shaping until sleeve is 18½ (19, 19, 19¼, 19¼) in / 47 (48, 48, 49, 49) cm long.

Shape Armhole: BO 5 sts, knit until 5 sts rem, BO 5 sts. Now work back and forth. BO 2 sts at beginning of next 2 rows and then decrease 1 st at beginning of each of next 10 rows. Continue without further shaping until sleeve cap measures 5¼ in / 13 cm. BO 4 sts at beginning of each of next 8 rows and then BO rem sts. Set first sleeve aside and make second sleeve the same way.

FINISHING

Join shoulders.

Front Bands: With smaller circular, pickup and knit 36 sts beginning at lower edge of right front, up to end of pattern panel; pm. Pick up and knit 75 (78, 81, 84, 87) sts from marker up to beginning of V-neck; pm. Pick up and knit 66 (68, 70, 72, 74) sts from marker up to shoulder seam. Pick up and knit 53 (56, 59, 61, 64) sts across back neck. Pick up and knit the same number of sts down left front as for up right front. Work 1 row k1tbl on WS. Continue back and forth in garter st (knit every row).

Buttonholes: On 5th row, work buttonholes: K36 to first marker on right front, k2 (3, 4, 5, 6), BO 3 sts, *k10, BO 3 sts*; rep * to * 4 more times = 6 buttonholes. Knit to end of row. On next row, CO 3 sts over each gap. Knit 4 more rows and then BO.

Weave in all ends neatly on WS. Gently steam press on WS under damp pressing cloth.

Sew on buttons to match buttonholes.

Attach sleeves.

CHART

NOTES REGARDING CHART: The pattern moves sideways by working 3tog and making 2 yarnovers on each repeat. Therefore, on the chart, the knit and purl sts are not always worked over each other, as drawn in. Work each round/row as shown so the pattern will come out correctly.

Symbols Key

⌐	K2tog
•	Purl
☐	Knit
ŏ	Yo
⋀	Sl 1, k2tog, psso
⌐	K2tog tbl

LEAF

This sweater is slightly shaped at the sides for a dressy A-line that suits most body types. The round-knitted yoke doesn't need much finishing, and the lacy neckband is loose and airy.

SKILL LEVEL
Intermediate to Experienced

SIZES
S (M, L, XL, XXL)

FINISHED MEASUREMENTS
Chest: 34 (36¼, 38½, 43, 46) in / 86 (92, 98, 109, 117) cm
Lower Edge, Circumference: 38½ (41, 43¼, 47¼, 51¼) in / 98 (104, 110, 120, 130) cm
Total Length: 24 (24¾, 25½, 26½, 27¼) in / 61 (63, 65, 67, 69) cm
Sleeve Length: 18½ (18½, 19, 19, 19¼) in / 47 (47, 48, 48, 49) cm

MATERIALS
Yarn:
CYCA #1 (fingering) HIllesvåg Sølje (100% Norwegian wool, 383 yd/350 m / 100 g)
and
CYCA #1 (fingering) HIllesvåg Vilje (100% Norwegian wool, 410 yd/375 m / 100 g)
Yarn Colors and Amounts:
Color 1: Sølje:
Blue Jeans 2113: 350 (350, 400, 400, 450) g
Color 2: Vilje:
Unbleached 400: 50 (50, 100, 100, 100) g
Needles: U. S. size 2.5 / 3 mm circulars and sets of 5 dpn. If you work two-color stranded knitting more tightly than one-color knitting, use U. S. 4 / 3.5 mm for those sections. Cable needle.

GAUGE
25 sts in stockinette/pattern with gauge-size needles = 4 in / 10 cm.
Adjust needle size to obtain correct gauge if necessary.

BODY

The body is worked in the round from the bottom up. With Color 1 and U. S. 2.5 / 3 mm circular, CO 246 (264, 276, 300, 324) sts. Join, being careful not to twist cast-on row. Pm for beginning of rnd. Knit 6 rnds in stockinette, purl 1 rnd = rolled edge. Change to circular needed to obtain gauge in two-color knitting and work in pattern following Chart II, working rep around and 1 rep in length. Continue in stockinette with Color 1.

Divide for front and back: Pm at each side = 123 (132, 138, 150, 162) sts each for front and back. Knit around for 1¼ in / 3 cm.

Shape sides: K1, k2tog, knit until 3 sts rem before next marker, k2tog tbl, k1 = front. Decrease the same way on back = 4 sts decreased on rnd. Decrease the same way every 1½ in / 4 cm a total of 7 (7, 7, 8, 8) times = 218 (236, 248, 268, 292) sts rem. Knit without further decreasing until body measures 15¾ (16¼, 16½, 16½, 17) in / 40 (41, 42, 42, 43) cm.

Shape Armholes: BO 8 sts at each side as follows: BO 4 sts, knit until 4 st before next marker, BO 8 sts, knit until 4 sts rem on rnd, BO 4 sts. Set body aside while you knit sleeves.

SLEEVES

The sleeves are knitted in the round. With Color 2 and dpn U. S. 2.5 / 3 mm, CO 42 (42, 48, 54, 60) sts. Divide sts onto dpn and join. Knit 6 rnds in stockinette, purl 1 rnd = rolled edge. Change to dpn needed to obtain gauge in two-color knitting and work in pattern following Chart II, working 1 rep around and 1 rep in length. Continue in Color 1 and stockinette, and, on first rnd, increase 0 (4, 2, 4, 4) sts evenly spaced around = 42 (46, 50, 58, 64) sts.

Shape Sleeve: On every 5th rnd, increase 2 sts centered on underarm until there are 84 (90, 96, 102, 112) sts. Continue straight up until sleeve is 18½ (18½, 19, 19, 19¼) in / 47 (47, 48, 48, 49) cm long.

Shape Armholes: BO 4 sts, knit until 4 sts rem, BO 4 sts. Set first sleeve aside and make second sleeve the same way.

JOINING BODY AND SLEEVES

Place all pieces on circular: front, right sleeve, back, left sleeve = 354 (384, 408, 440, 484) sts total. Pm at each intersection of body and sleeve = 4 markers.

Knit 2 rnds, and on 2nd rnd decrease/increase as follows:

Increase 2 (decrease 2, decrease 8, decrease 6, increase 2) sts evenly spaced around = 356 (382, 400, 434, 486) sts.

Raglan Shaping: Knit until 2 sts before first marker, k2tog tbl, sl m, k2tog. Decrease the same way at each marker. Decrease the same way on every rnd 4 (5, 5, 7, 9) times = 324 (342, 360, 378, 414) sts rem. Now work in pattern following Chart I, working 18 (19, 20, 21, 23) rep around. Work 1 rep in length.

NOTE: You will decrease as you work charted pattern. After pattern is complete, 126 (133, 140, 147, 161) sts rem.

Knit 2 rnds with Color 1 and then decrease 6 (7, 8, 9, 10) sts evenly spaced around. BO rem sts.

Neckband: With Color 1 and dpn or short circular U. S. 2.5 / 3 mm, pick up and knit 133 (133, 133, 152, 152) sts around neck. Work 1 rnd k1tbl, purl 1 rnd. Turn work so you will continue with WS facing; this way, the collar will fold to the outside when finished. Work in pattern following Chart III, working 7 (7, 7, 8, 8) rep around. Work Rows 1-10 of Chart III 3 times, and then Rows 11-24 once and Rows 25-34 2 times.

Garter Stitch Edging:
Knit 1 rnd, purl 1 rnd with Color 1.
Knit 1 rnd, purl 1 rnd with Color 2.
Knit 1 rnd, purl 1 rnd with Color 1.
Knit 1 rnd, purl 1 rnd with Color 2.
Seam underarms.

FINISHING

Weave in all ends neatly on WS. Gently steam press sweater on WS under a damp pressing cloth.

CHART I

CHART II

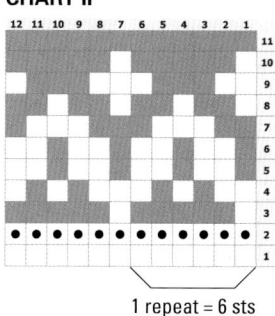

1 repeat = 6 sts

Symbols Key for Charts I and II

■	Knit with Color 1
□	Knit with Color 2
•	Purl with Color 2

1 repeat = 18 sts

Symbols Key for Chart III

□	Knit
•	Purl
⟋	K2tog
ᐭ	Yo
■	No stitch—the st has been decreased away
⟍	K2tog tbl
⤬⤬	Place 2 sts on cable needle and hold in front of work, k2, k2 from cable needle

CHART III

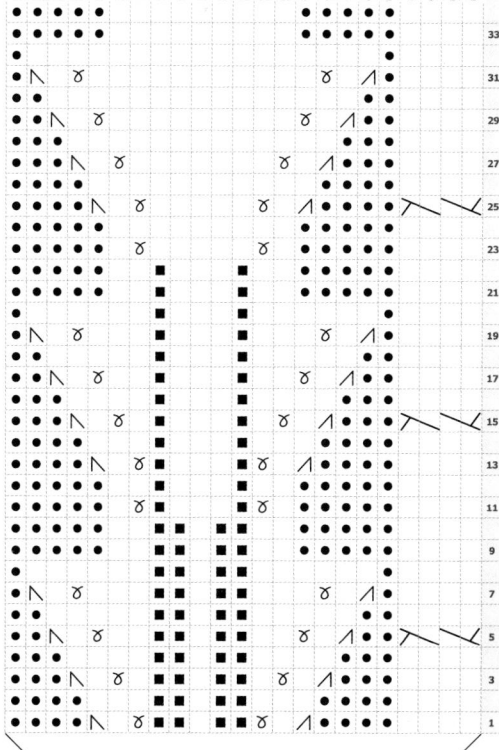

1 repeat = 23 sts

INANNA

This jacket is named for Inanna, which means "Queen of Heaven." She was one of the most important goddesses in old Mesopotamia. The jacket is knitted in delicate colors with gold yarn for the edgings: a true queen.

SKILL LEVEL
Intermediate to Experienced

SIZES
S (M, L, XL, XXL)

FINISHED MEASUREMENTS
Chest: 34¾ (37, 40¼, 44, 48¾) in / 88 (94, 102, 112, 124) cm
Total Length: 22 (22¾, 23¾, 24½, 25¼) in / 56 (58, 60, 62, 64) cm
Sleeve Length: 19 (19¼, 19¼, 19¾, 19¾) in / 48 (49, 49, 50, 50) cm

MATERIALS
Yarn:
CYCA #2 (sport, baby) Hillesvåg Ask/Hifa 2 (100% Norwegian wool, 344 yd/315 m / 100 g)
and
CYCA #1 (fingering) Rauma Concorde (64% rayon, 36% polyester, 137 yd/125 m / 25 g)

Yarn Colors and Amounts:
Ask:
Color 1: Purple Beige 6101: 150 (200, 200, 250, 250) g
Color 2: Light Pink Heather 6574: 200 (200, 250, 250, 300) g
Color 3: Dark Brown Heather 6103: 50 (50, 50, 100, 100) g
Color 4: Beige 61001: 50 (50, 100, 100, 100) g
Concorde:
Color 5: Gold 20: 25 (25, 25, 25, 25) g (hold double when knitting or crocheting)
Needles: U. S. sizes 1.5 and 2.5 / 2.5 and 3 mm circulars and sets of 5 dpn.
If you work two-color stranded knitting more tightly than one-color knitting, use U. S. 4 / 3.5 mm for those sections.
Crochet Hook: U. S. B-1 or C-2 / 2.5 mm
Notions: 11 buttons to match cardigan color; approx. 1.4 yd / 1.3 m ribbon to cover cut steek edges

GAUGE
24 sts and 25 rnds in stockinette/pattern with larger needles = 4 in / 10 cm.
Adjust needle size to obtain correct gauge if necessary.

BODY

The body is worked in the round from the bottom up. With Color 3 and smaller circular, CO 209 (225, 249, 269, 297) sts + 6 steek sts at center front.

Steek: Purl steek sts; do not include steek sts in stitch counts. To make cutting and sewing later easier, and to secure the yarns, work the 2 center sts with pattern color.

Join, being careful not to twist cast-on row. Pm for beginning of rnd. Knit 7 rnds in stockinette. Change to Color 5, with yarn held double, and knit 1 rnd, purl 1 rnd = foldline. Pm as follows: Count 52 (56, 62, 67, 74) sts for right front, pm, 105 (113, 125, 135, 149) sts for back, pm, 52 (56, 62, 67, 74) sts for right front. Make sure the 6 steek sts are at center front. Work in pattern following Chart I, beginning at arrow for right front; work pattern to side marker. Begin at arrow for your size on back, and work pattern over back. The left front is worked mirror-image to correspond to right front. Work 1 rep in length. Change to larger circular (size needed to obtain gauge for two-color knitting) and work in pattern following Chart II. Work 1 rep in length. Now work pattern following Chart III, beginning at arrow for your size. Work until body measures approx. 13¾ in / 35 cm from foldline and you are on Row 5 of Chart III.

Shape Armholes: On Row 6 of Chart III, BO 8 sts at each side for armholes: Knit until 4 sts before first side marker, BO 8 sts, knit until 4 sts before next side marker, BO 8 sts, knit to end of rnd. Set body aside while you knit sleeves.

SLEEVES

The sleeves are knitted in the round. With Color 3 and smaller dpn, CO 52 (52, 58, 58, 66) sts. Divide sts onto dpn and join. Knit 7 rnds in stockinette. Change to Color 5, with yarn held double, and knit 1 rnd, purl 1 rnd = foldline.

Pattern on Sleeve: Work in pattern following Chart I for 1 rep in length. See arrow for center of sleeve and count back to determine beginning st of rnd. Work 1 rep in length.

NOTE: See "Shape Sleeve" section below for increases beginning after Chart I.

Work pattern following Chart II for 1 rep in length. See arrow for center of sleeve and count back to determine beginning st of rnd. Work from Chart III pattern for rest of sleeve.

Shape Sleeve: After completing Chart I, on every 5th rnd, increase 2 sts centered on underarm until there are 92 (96, 100, 110, 118) sts. Continue straight up until sleeve is 19 (19¼, 19¼, 19¾, 19¾) in / 48 (49, 49, 50, 50) cm long and you are on Row 5 of Chart III. On Row 6 of Chart III, BO 4 sts. Knit until 4 sts rem, BO 4 sts. Set first sleeve aside while you knit second sleeve the same way.

JOINING BODY AND SLEEVES

Place all pieces on larger circular: front, right sleeve, back, left sleeve + steek = 361 (385, 417, 457, 501) sts total + 6 steek sts. Pm at each intersection of body and sleeve = 4 markers.

Continue in pattern following Chart III. On 2nd rnd in pattern, begin raglan shaping.

Raglan Shaping: Knit until 2 sts before first marker, k2tog tbl, sl m, k2tog. Decrease the same way at each marker. Decrease the same way on every rnd 5 (6, 6, 8, 9) times = 321 (337, 369, 393, 429) sts rem. Now work raglan shaping on every other rnd a total of 25 (26, 27, 30, 34) times and then on every rnd 3 times. After you've worked approx. 4 in / 10 cm from joining of body and sleeves and you are on Row 6 of Chart III, change to pattern on Chart IV for the rest of the work. Begin with Rows 1-6 of Chart IV and then rep Rows 7-12. BO all sts.

FINISHING

Weave in all ends neatly on WS. Gently steam press sweater on WS under a damp pressing cloth. Machine-stitch 2 lines, zigzag and straight stitch, on each side of center front sts. Carefully cut open up center of steek. Seam underarms.

Neckband: With larger circular and Color 2, pick up and knit 115 (121, 127, 133, 133) sts around neck. Work 1 rnd k1tbl and then work 1 rep in length of pattern following Chart I, beginning with 1st st on chart. Change to Color 5 and doubled yarn, knit 2 rnds = foldline. Knit 8 rnds in stockinette. BO. Fold band doubled to WS and sew down neatly.

Left Front Band: With crochet hook and Color 4, work 1 row sc along left front edge; turn and work 1 row sc back. Change to Color 2 and work 2 rows sc. Change to Color 1 and work 2 rows sc + 1 row picot: *1 sc, ch 3, 1 sc in first ch, 2 sc*; rep * to * across. Cut yarn and fasten off.

Right Front Band: Mark placement of 11 buttons on left band, with top one ⅜ in / 1 cm from top edge and lowest ⅜ in / 1 cm above lower foldline. Crochet edging as for left band, but on Row 3, make buttonholes: ch 4, skip 3 sc and work 1 sc in next

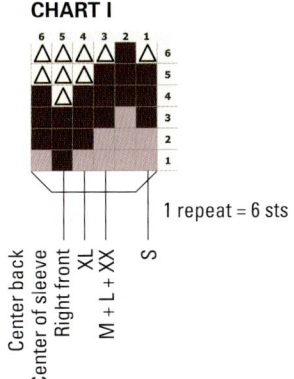

CHART I

1 repeat = 6 sts

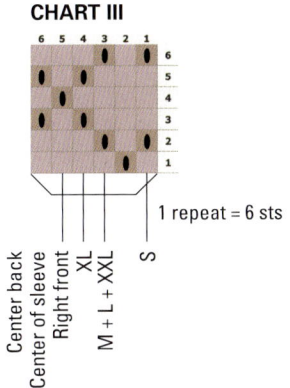

CHART III

1 repeat = 6 sts

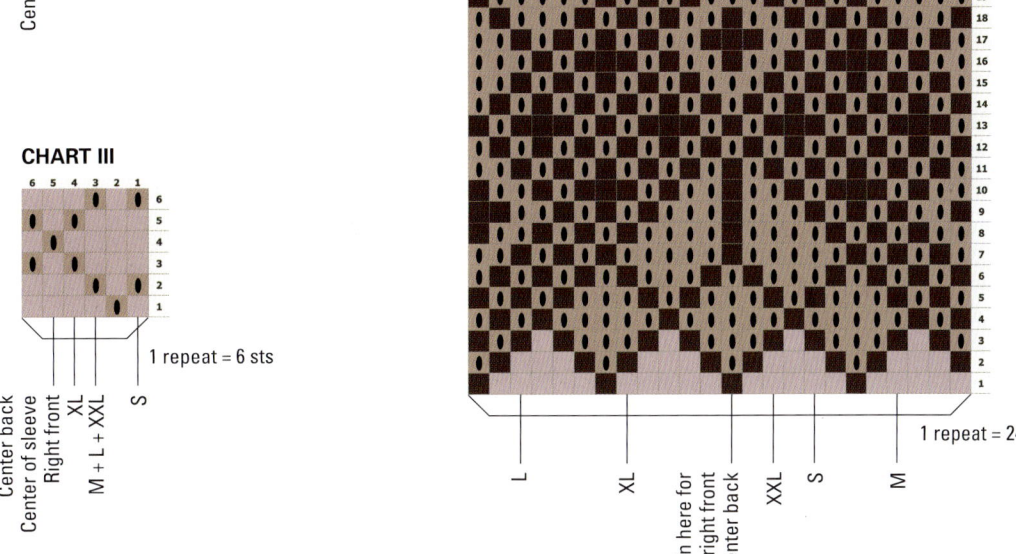

CHART II

1 repeat = 24 sts

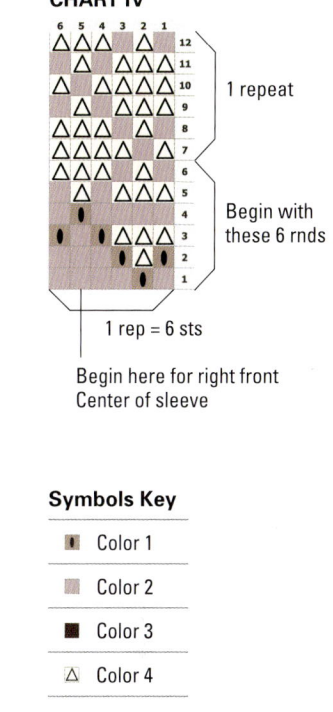

CHART IV

1 repeat = 6 sts

Begin with these 6 rnds

Begin here for right front
Center of sleeve

Symbols Key

- Color 1
- Color 2
- Color 3
- △ Color 4

sc. On next row, work 3 sc around each ch-4 loop.

Edging on Collar and Sleeve Cuffs: With crochet hook and Color 5, work 1 row sc along foldline of collar. Work 1 row of picots as for front bands. Crochet the same way around lower edge of each sleeve.

Weave in all ends neatly on WS. Sew on buttons spaced as for buttonholes.

Sew ribbon on back of front bands to cover cut steek edges.

GLASTONBURY

The pattern on the yoke of this pullover was inspired by stained glass windows in cathedrals I have visited around the world. The pullover has ribbed edges, combined with garter stitch stripes in colors from the yoke at the lower edges of the body and sleeves.

SKILL LEVEL
Intermediate to Experienced

SIZES
S (M, L, XL, XXL)

FINISHED MEASUREMENTS
Chest: 35½ (38½, 41¾, 48¾, 54¼) in / 90 (98, 106, 124, 138) cm
Total Length: 24½ (24¾, 25¼, 26, 26¾) in / 62 (63, 64, 66, 68) cm
Sleeve Length: 19 (19, 19¼, 19¼, 19¼) in / 48 (48, 49, 49, 49) cm

MATERIALS
Yarn:
CYCA #1 (fingering) Hillesvåg Vilje (100% Norwegian wool, 410 yd/375 m / 100 g)
and
CYCA #1 (fingering) Hillesvåg Sølje (100% Norwegian wool, 383 yd/350 m / 100 g)

Yarn Colors and Amounts:
Vilje:
Color 1: Unbleached 400: 250 (250, 300, 350, 400) g
Sølje:
Color 2: Lime 2107: 50 (50, 50, 50, 50) g
Color 3: Red 2132: 50 (50, 50, 50, 50) g
Color 4: Cognac 2103: 50 (50, 50, 50, 50) g
Color 5: Burgundy 2104: 50 (50, 50, 50, 50) g
Needles: U. S. sizes 1.5 and 2.5 / 2.5 and 3 mm circulars and sets of 5 dpn.
If you work two-color stranded knitting more tightly than one-color knitting, use U. S. 4 / 3.5 mm for those sections.

GAUGE
25 sts in stockinette/pattern with larger needles = 4 in / 10 cm.
Adjust needle size to obtain correct gauge if necessary.

Knitting Tip: Don't forget to twist the colors around each other when there are more than 5 stitches between color changes.

CHART

Symbols Key

- ☐ Color 1
- ▽ Color 2
- ✚ Color 3
- ⬬ Color 4
- ◆ Color 5
- ■ No st—st has been decreased away
- ⋉ K2tog with color indicated

1 repeat = 20 sts

BODY

The body is worked in the round from the bottom up. With Color 1 and smaller circular, CO 224 (244, 264, 308, 344) sts. Join, being careful not to twist cast-on row; pm for beginning of rnd and at side, with same number of sts for front and back. Work around in k2tbl, p2 ribbing for 12 rnds. Change to larger circular and Color 4. Knit 1 rnd, purl 1 rnd. Change to Color 3 and knit 1 rnd, purl 1 rnd. Change to Color 5 and knit 1 rnd, purl 1 rnd. Change to Color 1 and knit around in stockinette until body measures 15½ in / 39 cm.

Shape Armholes: BO 12 (12, 12, 12, 14) sts at each side as follows: BO 6 (6, 6, 6, 7) sts, knit until 6 (6, 6, 6, 7) sts before next side marker, BO 12 (12, 12, 12, 14) sts, knit until 6 (6, 6, 6, 7) sts before next side marker, BO 6 (6, 6, 6, 7) sts. Set body aside while you knit sleeves.

SLEEVES

The sleeves are worked in the round. With Color 1 and smaller dpn, CO 56 (56, 60, 60, 66) sts. Divide sts onto dpn and join. Work around in k2tbl, p2 ribbing for 12 rnds. Change to large size dpn and Color 4. Knit 1 rnd, purl 1 rnd. Change to Color 3 and knit 1 rnd, purl 1 rnd. Change to Color 5 and knit 1 rnd, purl 1 rnd. Change to Color 1 and continue around in stockinette.

Shape Sleeve: Increase 2 sts at center of underarm on every 8th rnd until there are 84 (92, 100, 108, 120) sts. Continue without further increasing until sleeve is 19 (19, 19¼, 19¼, 19¼) in / 48 (48, 49, 49, 49) cm long.

Next Rnd: BO 6 (6, 6, 6, 7) sts, knit until 6 (6, 6, 6, 7) sts rem and BO those sts.

Set first sleeve aside while you knit second sleeve the same way.

JOINING BODY AND SLEEVES

Place all pieces on larger circular: front, right sleeve, back, left sleeve = 344 (380, 416, 476, 528) sts total. Pm at each intersection of body and sleeve = 4 markers.

Knit 1 rnd with Color 1, decreasing 0 (0, 0, 0, 4) sts evenly spaced around = 344 (380, 416, 476, 524) sts.

Raglan Shaping: Knit until 2 sts before first marker, k2tog tbl, sl m, k2tog. Decrease the same way at each marker. Decrease the same way on every rnd 3 (5, 7, 7, 8) times =

320 (340, 360, 420, 460) sts rem.
Yoke Pattern: Raglan shaping is complete. Additional shaping is worked into yoke pattern. Change to larger needle if necessary to obtain gauge for two-color stranded knitting. Work in pattern following chart = 16 (17, 18, 21, 23) rep around. Work entire chart repeat in length = 112 (119, 126, 147, 157) sts rem. BO rem sts.

FINISHING

Weave in all ends neatly on WS. Gently steam press sweater on WS under a damp pressing cloth. Seam underarms.
Neckband: With smaller circular and Color 5, pick up and knit 112 (118, 122, 138, 148) sts around neck and work 1 rnd k1tbl, then purl 1 rnd. Change to Color 3 and knit 1 rnd, purl 1 rnd. Change to Color 4 and knit 1 rnd, purl 1 rnd. Change to Color 1 and (knit 1 rnd, purl 1 rnd) 2 times. BO all sts.

FRIDA'S
MEXICAN JACKET

A colorful and life-affirming jacket inspired by the Mexican artist Frida Kahlo. The jacket is knitted in the round with set-in sleeves, a pretty shawl collar, and colorful motifs with knit and purl stitches.

SKILL LEVEL
Experienced

SIZES
S (M, L, XL, XXL)

FINISHED MEASUREMENTS
Chest: 44 (47¼, 49¾, 52½, 55½) in / 112 (120, 126, 133, 141) cm
Total Length: approx. 32¼ (32¾, 33, 33½, 34) in / 82 (83, 84, 85, 86) cm
Sleeve Length: 18¼ (18½, 18½, 19, 19) in / 46 (47, 47, 48, 48) cm
The jacket is oversized—check measurements to determine the size you want.

MATERIALS
Yarn:
CYCA #5 (bulky) Hillesvåg Blåne (100% wool, 125 yd/114 m / 100 g)
Yarn Colors and Amounts:
Color 1: Navy Blue 2133: 1,000 (1,000, 1,100, 1,100, 1,200) g
Color 2: Deep Rose 2114: 100 (100, 100, 100, 100) g
Color 3: Cognac 2103: 100 (100, 100, 100, 100) g
Color 4: Lime 2107: 100 (100, 100, 100, 100) g
Color 5: Red 2132: 100 (100, 200, 200, 200) g
Color 6: Red-Gold 2122: 100 (100, 200, 200, 200) g
Needles: U. S. sizes 9 and 10 / 5.5 and 6 mm circulars and sets of 5 dpn. You'll need a long circular in a smaller size for the collar.
If you work two-color stranded knitting more tightly than one-color knitting, go up a needle size for those sections.
Notions: 7 buttons to match jacket; approx. 2.2 yd / 2 m pretty ribbon to cover cut steek edges

GAUGE
14 sts and 22 rnds in stockinette/pattern with larger needles = 4 in / 10 cm.
Adjust needle size to obtain correct gauge if necessary.

NOTES: Don't forget to twist the colors around each other when there are more than 5 stitches between color changes.
Read through the pattern fully before you begin to knit. There are several places where some steps occur simultaneously. Mark each occurrence of "*at the same time*" so you will be aware of these simultaneous steps.

BODY

With smaller circular and Color 1, CO 157 (167, 177, 187, 197) sts. Work back and forth. Knit 1 row, purl 1 row, knit 2 rows, purl 2 rows = rolled lower edge.

Join to work in the round: CO 4 sts for steek at center front.

Steek: Purl steek sts with Color 1 throughout; do not include steek sts in stitch counts.

Change to larger circular for two-color knitting and work around in pattern following Chart I. See arrow for your size for beginning st. Work Rows 1-20 of chart and then rep Rows 21-32 (lice) until jacket measures approx. 12¾ in / 32 cm. Make sure you end on Row 26 or 32 of Chart I.

Now work in pattern following Chart II, beginning at arrow for your size. Continue in pattern until body measures 22 (22½, 22¾, 23¼, 23¾) in / 56 (57, 58, 59, 60) cm. Divide with 37 (40, 42, 45, 47) sts for each front and 83 (87, 93, 97, 103) sts for back. Pm between each piece and work each separately.

Back: Work back and forth in pattern following Chart II, completing chart in length and then repeating Rows 53-62. When 1½ in / 4 cm before total length, BO the center 23 (23, 25, 25, 25) sts for back neck. Work each side separately. Work 4 rows in pattern, and *at the same time*, on every other row, decrease 1 st at neck edge 2 times. BO rem sts for shoulder. Work opposite side of neck to correspond.

Front: BO the 4 steek sts and work each front separately.

Right Front: Continue back and forth in pattern. *At the same time*, begin shaping V-neck on right side of piece. Pm where V-neck begins. On every 4th row, decrease 1 st 11 (12, 12, 13, 12) times. Continue until front is same length as back. BO rem sts.

Left Front: Work to correspond to right front.

SLEEVES

With smaller dpn and Color 1, CO 39 (41, 43, 45, 47) sts. Work back and forth. Knit 1 row, purl 1 row, knit 2 rows, purl 2 rows = rolled lower edge.

Join to work in the round. Change to larger dpn and work in pattern following Chart I. See arrow for center of sleeve and count back to determine beginning st for your size.

Continue in pattern, and at the same time, shape sleeve:

Pattern: Work Rows 1-20 of Chart I around. Then rep Rows 21-32 (lice) for rest of sleeve.

Shape Sleeve: *At the same time* as beginning pattern, increase 2 sts at center of underarm on every 4th rnd until there are 67 (69, 71, 73, 75) sts. Work new sts into pattern. When sleeve is 18¼ (18½, 18½, 19, 19) in / 46 (47, 47, 48, 48) cm long, BO all sts. Set first sleeve aside while you knit second sleeve the same way.

FINISHING

Weave in all ends neatly on WS. Gently steam press sweater on WS under a damp pressing cloth.
Join shoulders.
Machine-stitch 2 lines, zigzag and straight stitch, on each side of center front steek sts. Carefully cut open up center of steek.

Front Bands and Shawl Collar: With Color 1 and smaller long circular, pick up and knit 115 (117, 118, 120, 122) sts along edge of right front, pm, 32 (34, 34, 34, 34) across back neck, pm, 115 (117, 118, 120, 122) sts along edge of left front. Work 1 row k1tbl on WS. Purl 1 row on RS and then work 2 rows in k2, p2 ribbing, ending row with k2.

Buttonholes: Mark spacing for 7 buttonholes on right front band, with lowest 2 sts from lower edge and top one at base of V-neck. For each buttonhole: On RS, k2tog, yo twice, k2tog tbl. Work 1 row with buttonholes on RS.

Shawl Collar: On next row (WS), begin working shawl collar. Work in ribbing to marker at base of V-neck on right front; turn and work back, slipping 1st st to right needle. Tug yarn slightly to prevent a hole at turn. Work to marker for V-neck on left front; turn and work back (each time you turn, slip 1st st over to right needle).

Work until 4 sts rem to marker on right front. Turn and work until 4 sts rem to marker on left front.

Work until 8 sts rem to marker on right front. Turn and work until 8 sts rem to marker on left front.

Work until 12 sts rem to marker on right front. Turn and work until 12 sts rem to marker on left front.

Work until 16 sts rem to marker on right front. Turn and work until 16 sts rem to marker on left front.

Work until 20 sts rem to marker on right front. Turn and work until 20 sts rem to marker on left front.

Work until 24 sts rem to marker on right front. Turn and work until 24 sts rem to marker on left front.

Work until 28 sts rem to marker on right front. Turn and work until 28 sts rem to marker on left front.

Work until 32 sts rem to marker on right front.

Turn and work to end of row.

CHART I

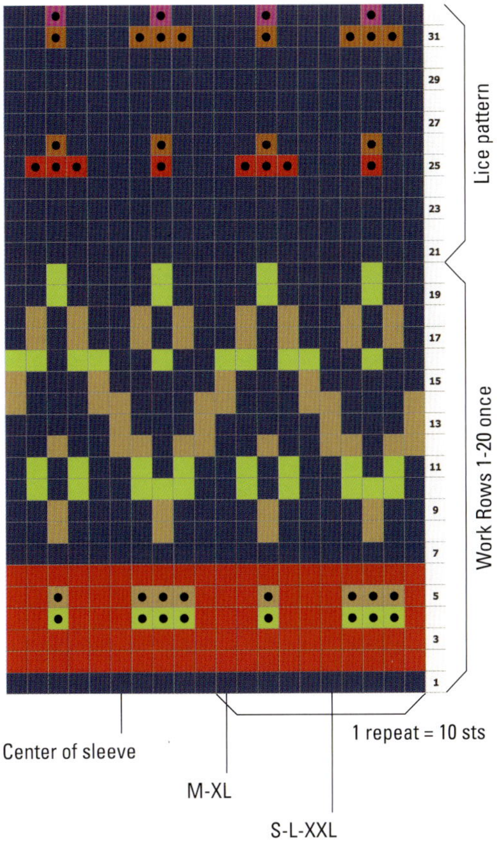
31
29
27
25
23
21
19
17
15
13
11
9
7
5
3
1
Lice pattern
Work Rows 1-20 once
1 repeat = 10 sts
Center of sleeve
M-XL
S-L-XXL

CHART II

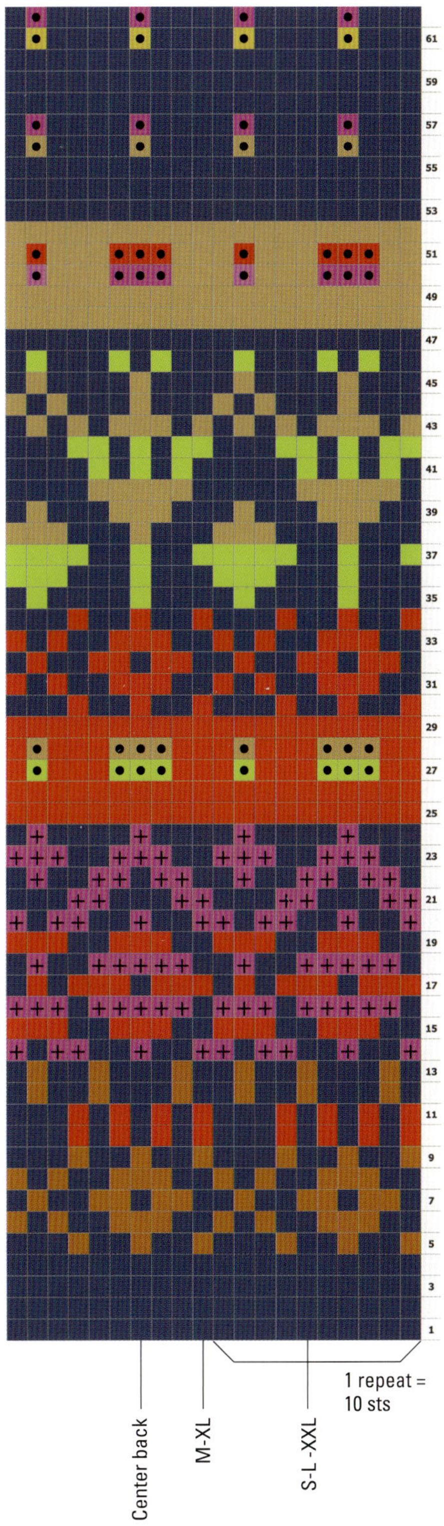
61
59
57
55
53
51
49
47
45
43
41
39
37
35
33
31
29
27
25
23
21
19
17
15
13
11
9
7
5
3
1
1 repeat = 10 sts
Center back
M-XL
S-L-XXL

Symbols Key

- Knit on RS, purl on WS with Color 1
- Knit on RS, purl on WS with Color 2
- Purl on RS, knit on WS with Color 2
- Knit on RS, purl on WS with Color 3
- Purl on RS, knit on WS with Color 3
- Knit on RS, purl on WS with Color 4
- Purl on RS, knit on WS with Color 4
- Knit on RS, purl on WS with Color 5
- Purl on RS, knit on WS with Color 5
- Knit on RS, purl on WS with Color 6
- Purl on RS, knit on WS with Color 6

On next row (WS), work entire row, *at the same time* knitting yarnovers in buttonholes as k1tbl. Work 4 rows in ribbing and end with 1 row on WS. BO in ribbing.

Attach sleeves.

Sew on buttons spaced as for buttonholes.

Sew ribbon to cover cut edges from steek on each front band.

BONBON

CABLED PULLOVER

A classic sweater with a combination of cables and wide ribbing. This pullover has a straight silhouette and set-in sleeves, and it's easy to knit. Best of all, the suggested yarn has a wide range of colors, so you can make it in your personal favorite.

SKILL LEVEL
Intermediate

SIZES
S (M, L, XL, XXL)

FINISHED MEASUREMENTS
Chest: 35½ (37, 38½, 40¼, 46½) in / 90 (94, 98, 102, 118) cm
Total Length: 22 (22¾, 23¾, 24½, 25¼) in / 56 (58, 60, 62, 64) cm
Sleeve Length: 19 (19, 19, 19¼, 19¾) in / 48 (48, 48, 49, 50) cm

MATERIALS
Yarn:
CYCA #3 (DK, light worsted) Rowan Felted Tweed (50% Merino wool, 25% alpaca, 25% viscose, 191 yd/175 m / 50 g)
Yarn Colors and Amounts:
Pink Bliss 199: 350 (350, 400, 400, 450) g
Needles: U. S. size 4 / 3.5 mm: circular and set of 5 dpn; cable needle

GAUGE
27 sts 29 rnds in cable pattern = 4 x 4 in / 10 x 10 cm.
22 sts 29 rnds in stockinette = 4 x 4 in / 10 x 10 cm.
Adjust needle size to obtain correct gauge if necessary.

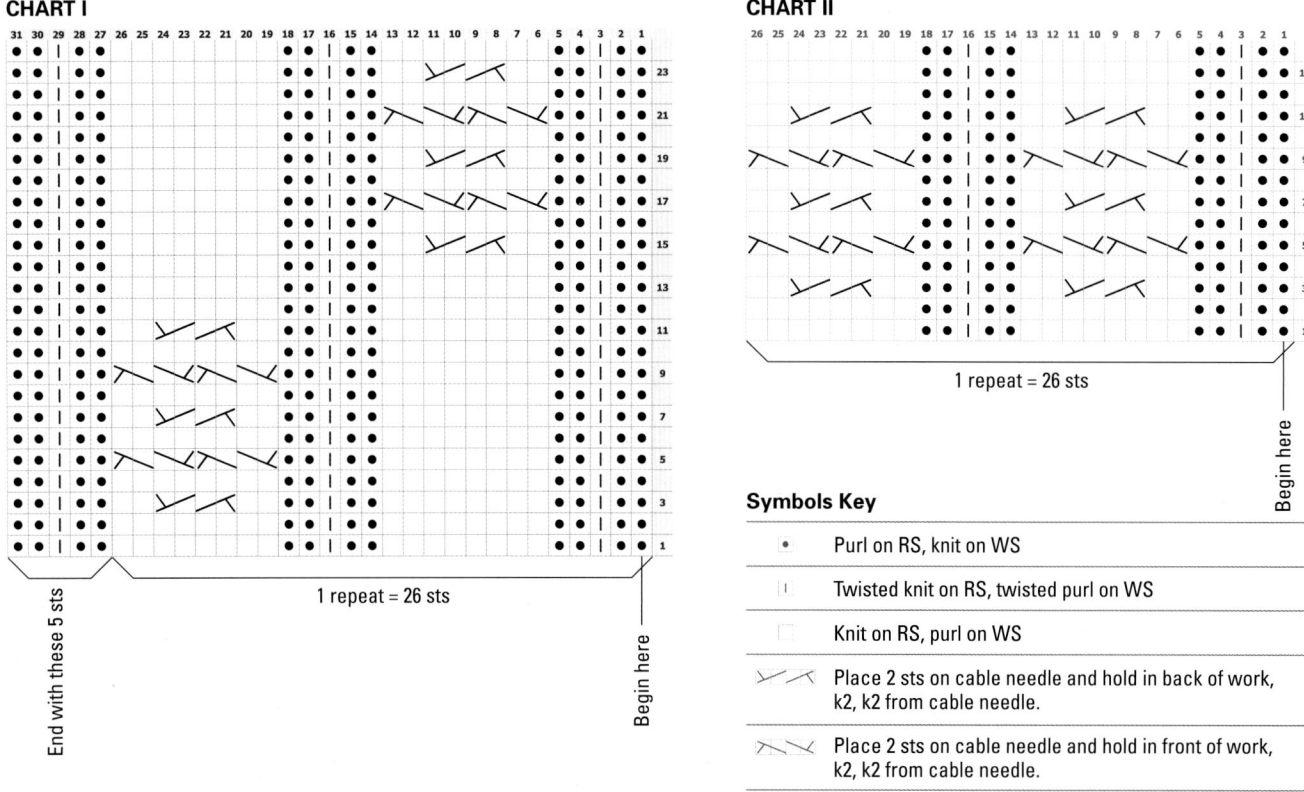

Symbols Key

•	Purl on RS, knit on WS
I	Twisted knit on RS, twisted purl on WS
☐	Knit on RS, purl on WS
⟩⟨	Place 2 sts on cable needle and hold in back of work, k2, k2 from cable needle.
⟨⟩	Place 2 sts on cable needle and hold in front of work, k2, k2 from cable needle.

BODY

The body is knitted in the round from the bottom up. With circular, CO 244 (252, 264, 278, 286) sts. Join, being careful not to twist cast-on row; pm for beginning of rnd.

Work cables as:

Front: K0 (2, 5, 2, 4); work in pattern following Chart I over 117 (117, 117, 130, 130) sts, ending with last 5 sts on chart and k0 (2, 5, 2, 4). Place side marker.

Back: Work as for front.

Continue in pattern as est until body measures a total of 13 (13½, 13¾, 14¼, 13¾) in / 33 (34, 35, 36, 35) cm. Divide body at side marker = 122 (126, 132, 139, 143) sts each for front and back. Work each piece separately, back and forth.

BACK

Shape Armholes: At each side, BO 4 sts; on every other row, decrease 1 st 3 times, and then on every 4th row, 1 st 4 times.

Neck Shaping: When armhole depth is 8 (8¼, 8¾, 9½, 10¼) in / 20 (21, 22, 24, 26) cm, shape neck and shoulders *at the same time*: BO the center 36 (38, 40, 41, 43) sts. Work each side separately. At neck edge, on every other row, BO 2 sts 2 times.

Shoulder Shaping: On every other row, from outer edge of shoulder, BO 9-9-10 (9-10-10, 10-10-11, 11-11-12, 11-12-12) sts. No sts rem. Work opposite side to correspond.

FRONT

Work as for back, but shape neck at 4¾ in / 12 cm before total length.

Neck Shaping: BO the center 24 (26, 28, 29, 31) sts. Work each side separately. At neck edge, on every other row, BO 2 sts 2 times and 1 st 6 times. Shape shoulder as for back when 1¼ in / 3 cm before total length. No sts rem. Work opposite side to correspond.

SLEEVES

For all sizes, with dpn, CO 52 sts. Divide sts onto dpn and join. Work 2 rep following Chart II with 1 rep in length. Rep last rnd on chart for rest of sleeve, and *at the same time*, shape sleeve.

Shape Sleeve: On every 6th rnd, increase 2 sts centered on underarm until there are 74 (78, 82, 90, 94) sts. Work new sts into ribbing. When sleeve is 19 (19, 19, 19¼, 19¾) in / 48 (48, 48, 49, 50) cm long, divide sleeve at center of underarm and work back and forth. BO 4 sts at each side of sleeve. Then, on every other row, decrease 1 st 4 (4, 5, 6, 6) times. On every 4th row, decrease 1 st 2 times. BO 4 sts each at beginning of next 10 rows. BO rem sts. Knit second sleeve the same way.

FINISHING

Weave in all ends neatly on WS.

Gently steam press sweater on WS under a damp pressing cloth. Join shoulders.

Neckband: With circular, pick up and knit 74 (76, 78, 80, 82) sts along front neck and 40 (42, 44, 46, 48) sts along back neck. Work 1 rnd p1tbl, knit 10 rnds and then BO.

Attach sleeves.

ROSITA

TOP WITH LACE PATTERN

A light, summery top, knitted with the softest yarn in a delightful cashmere blend. The top has a lace panel at the lower edge of the body and rolled edges around the neck and sleeves.

SKILL LEVEL
Easy

SIZES
S (M, L, XL, XXL)

FINISHED MEASUREMENTS
Chest: 32¾ (35, 37½, 40¼, 45) in / 83 (89, 95, 102, 114) cm
Total Length: 20½ (21¼, 22, 22¾, 23¾) in / 52 (54, 56, 58, 60) cm

MATERIALS
Yarn:
CYCA #3 (DK, light worsted) Rowan Cashmere Tweed (80% Merino wool, 20% cashmere, 96 yd/88 m / 25 g)
You could also substitute a cotton yarn that knits at the same gauge.
Yarn Colors and Amounts:
Petal 00011: 175 (200, 200, 225, 250) g
Needles: U. S. sizes 2.5 and 4 / 3 and 3.5 mm: circulars; cable needle

GAUGE
22 sts in stockinette on larger needle = 4 in / 10 cm.
Adjust needle size to obtain correct gauge if necessary.

CHART

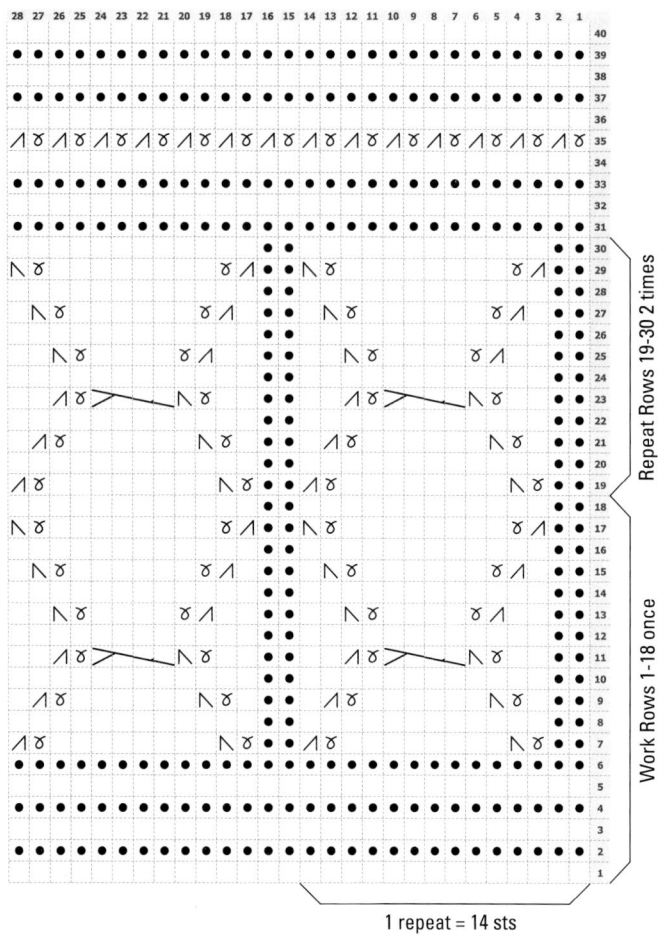

1 repeat = 14 sts

Symbols Key

☐	Knit on RS, purl on WS
•	Purl on RS, knit on WS
ଓ	Yo
⃥	K2tog tbl
⃫	K2tog
⤫	Place 2 sts on cable needle and hold in front of work, k2, k2 from cable needle

BODY

The body is worked in the round from the bottom up.
With smaller circular, CO 182 (196, 210, 224, 252) sts. Join, being careful not to twist cast-on row; pm for beginning of rnd. Work following chart, with 13 (14, 15, 16, 18) rep around. Work Rows 1-18 of chart once, Rows 19-30 2 times, and end with Rows 31-40. Change to larger circular. Work rest of body in stockinette.
When body measures 11½ (11¾, 12¼, 12¾, 13) in / 29 (30, 31, 32, 33) cm, divide for front and back = 91 (98, 105, 112, 126) sts each.
Back: Work back and forth in stockinette until 1½ in / 4 cm before total length.
Shape Shoulders: At each side, on every other row, BO 5-5-6-6 (6-6-6-7, 7-7-7-7, 7-8-8-8, 9-9-9-10) sts. *At the same time,* after 2 rows binding-off at each side, shape back neck: BO the center 39 (40, 41, 42, 44) sts and work each side separately. At neck edge, on every other row, BO 2 sts 2 times. No sts rem. Work opposite side to correspond.
Front: Work as for back but shape neck at 3½ in / 9 cm before total length. BO the center 23 (24, 25, 26, 28) sts for front neck. Work each side separately. At neck edge, on every other row, BO 2 sts 3 times and 1 st 6 times.
At the same time, shape shoulder as for back. Work opposite side to correspond.

FINISHING

Weave in all ends neatly on WS. *Gently* steam press sweater on WS under a damp pressing cloth. Join shoulders.
Neckband: With smaller circular, pick up and knit 71 (73, 75, 77, 79) sts along front neck and 46 (48, 50, 52, 54) sts along back neck. Work 1 rnd k1tbl, purl 1 rnd, knit 1 rnd, purl 1 rnd and then knit 4 rnds. BO.
Armhole Edgings: With smaller dpn, pick up and knit 83 (87, 91, 95, 99) sts around armhole. Work 1 rnd k1tbl, purl 1 rnd, knit 1 rnd , purl 1 rnd and then knit 4 rnds. BO.

MORNING RED

This colorful and fresh cardigan is inspired by colors of the sunrise here on Granavollen where I live. It has raglan shaping and ¾ length sleeves, and it's easy to knit.

SKILL LEVEL
Easy

SIZES
S (M, L, XL, XXL)

FINISHED MEASUREMENTS
Chest: 35½ (37½, 39¾, 44, 49¼) in / 90 (95, 101, 112, 125) cm
Total Length: approx. 23¼ (23¾, 24, 24¾, 25½) in / 59 (60, 61, 63, 65) cm
Sleeve Length: 13 (13, 13, 13, 13) in / 33 (33, 33, 33, 33) cm

MATERIALS
Yarn:
CYCA #3 (DK, light worsted) Rowan Felted Tweed (50% Merino wool, 25% alpaca, 25% viscose, 191 yd/175 m / 50 g)
Yarn Colors and Amounts:
Color 1: Treacle 145: 50 (50, 100, 100, 100) g
Color 2: Rage 150: 50 (50, 100, 100, 100) g
Color 3: Zinnia 198: 100 (100, 100, 100, 100) g
Color 4: Peony 183: 100 (100, 100, 100, 100) g
Color 5: Mineral 181: 50 (50, 50, 100, 100) g
Needles: U. S. sizes 2.5 and 4 / 3 and 3.5 mm: circulars and sets of 5 dpn
Notions: 7 buttons to match colors in cardigan

GAUGE
22 sts in stockinette on larger needles = 4 in / 10 cm. Adjust needle size to obtain correct gauge if necessary.

CHART

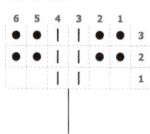

Center of sleeve

Symbols Key

□	Knit on RS, purl on WS with Color 1
I	Sl 1 with yarn held on WS with stripe color
•	Purl on RS and knit on WS with Color 1

NOTE: Read through the pattern fully before you begin to knit. There are several places where some steps occur simultaneously. Mark each occurrence of "*at the same time*" so you will be aware of these simultaneous steps.

Stripe Pattern:
18 rows Color 2 on body and 20 rnds on sleeves.
1 repeat following chart.
2 rows Color 3, 2 rows Color 2.
Rep from * to * 4 times and end with 2 rows Color 3.
1 repeat following chart.
18 rows Color 3 on body and 20

rnds on sleeves.
1 repeat following chart.
2 rows Color 4, 2 rows Color 3.
Rep from * to * 4 times and end with 2 rows Color 4.
1 repeat following chart.
18 rows Color 4 on body and 20 rnds on sleeves.
1 repeat following chart.
2 rows Color 5, 2 rows Color 4.
Rep from * to * 4 times and end with 2 rows Color 5.
1 repeat following chart.
Work rest of body/sleeves with Color 5.

BODY

The body is worked back and forth from the bottom up. With smaller circular and Color 1, CO 196 (208, 220, 244, 274) sts. Work 8 rows in twisted ribbing—on RS rows: K2tbl, p2; on WS rows: work purl sts as purl tbl and knit the knit sts. Change to larger circular and Color 2. Work 2 rows in stockinette, and *at the same time*, increase 1 st at beginning and end of 1st row = 198 (210, 222, 246, 276) sts. Pm at each side with 49 (52, 55, 61, 68) sts for each front and 100 (106, 112, 124, 140) sts for back.
Work pattern following chart, beginning on right side and repeating chart to end of row.
Stripe Pattern: Work stripe pattern in stockinette as explained above for rest of body. Work until body measures 13 in / 33 cm. Pm on row to indicate where you are in the stripe pattern.
Shape Armholes at Each Side: Work until 5 sts before first side marker, BO 10 sts; work until 5 sts before next side marker, BO 10 sts; work to end of row.

SLEEVES

The sleeves are worked in the round. With smaller dpn and Color 1, CO 48 (48, 52, 52, 56) sts. Divide sts onto dpn and join. Work 8 rnds k2tbl, p2 ribbing. Change to larger dpn and Color 2. Knit 2 rnds, and *at the same time*, on 1st rnd, increase 6 (8, 6, 8, 6) sts evenly spaced around = 54 (56, 58, 60, 62) sts.
Work in pattern following chart. See arrow for center of sleeve and count back to determine first st of rnd.
Stripe Pattern: Work stripe pattern in stockinette as explained above for rest of sleeve.
Shape Sleeve: At the same time, on every 5th rnd, increase 2 sts centered on underarm until there are 82 (86, 90, 96, 102) sts. When sleeve is 13 in / 33 cm long and on same row as body, shape armhole: BO first 5 sts, knit until 5 sts rem and BO 5 sts. Set first sleeve aside while you knit second sleeve the same way.

JOINING BODY AND SLEEVES

Read through this section fully before you begin knitting to make sure you are aware of all simultaneous steps.
Place all pieces on larger circular: right front, right sleeve, back, left sleeve, left front = 322 (342, 362, 398, 440) sts total. Pm at each intersection of body and sleeve = 4 markers. Continue working stripe pattern. On 2nd row, begin shaping raglan on RS:
Raglan Shaping: Knit until 2 sts before 1st marker, k2tog tbl, sl m, k2tog. Decrease the same way at each marker.
On WS, work the 2 sts before 1st marker as p2tog, then p2tog tbl. Decrease the same way at each marker.

Decrease as est on every rnd 3 (4, 5, 6, 8) times = 298 (310, 322, 350, 376) sts rem.
Now decrease for raglan as est on every other row 23 (24, 25, 28, 30) times and then on every row 3 times. *At the same time*, when 8 raglan decrease rows rem, and 178 (182, 186, 198, 208) sts rem, BO 10 (11, 12, 13, 14) sts at neck edge on each front. On each side of neck, on every other row, BO 2 sts once, and 1 st 2 (2, 3, 3, 4) times. Continue raglan shaping until all decrease rows are complete. BO rem sts.

FINISHING

Weave in all ends neatly on WS. Gently steam press sweater on WS under a damp pressing cloth.
Left Front Band: With smaller circular and Color 5, pick up and knit 120 (122, 124, 129, 134) sts along left front edge. Work 1 row p1tbl on WS and then work 1 rep following chart. Knit 1 row and BO.
Right Front Band: Mark spacing for 7 buttons on left front band, with top one 2 sts below top edge and bottom one 2 sts from beginning of band. Work edging as for left band, but on Row 3, make buttonholes: K2tog tbl, yo. On next row, work yarnover as k1tbl.
Neckband: With smaller circular and Color 5, pick up and knit 110 (114, 118, 122, 126) sts around neck and tops of front bands. Work 1 row p1tbl on WS and then work 1 rep following chart. Knit 1 row and BO. Sew on buttons spaced as for buttonholes.
Seam underarms.

GOLDEN DAYS

A loose-fitting pullover with garter stitch bands on the lower edges of the body and sleeves. The round yoke, in lovely tones of red and gold, is finished with a double rolled edging.

SKILL LEVEL
Intermediate

SIZES
S (M, L, XL, XXL)

FINISHED MEASUREMENTS
Chest: 39½ (43, 45¾, 48½, 52¾) in / 100 (109, 116, 123, 134) cm
Total Length: approx. 23¼ (23¾, 24, 24¾, 25½) in / 59 (60, 61, 63, 65) cm
Sleeve Length: 18¼ (18¼, 18½, 18½, 19) in / 46 (46, 47, 47, 48) cm

MATERIALS
Yarn:
CYCA #3 (DK, light worsted) Rowan Felted Tweed (50% Merino wool, 25% alpaca, 25% viscose, 191 yd/175 m / 50 g)

Yarn Colors and Amounts:
Color 1: Rage 150: 250 (300, 300, 350, 350) g
Color 2: Mineral 181: 50 (50, 50, 50, 50) g
Color 3: Pink Bliss 199: 50 (50, 50, 50, 50) g
Color 4: Zinnia 198: 50 (50, 50, 50, 50) g
Color 5: Treacle 145: 50 (50, 50, 50, 100) g
Needles: U. S. sizes 2.5 and 4 / 3 and 3.5 mm: circulars and sets of 5 dpn. If you work two-color stranded knitting more tightly than one-color knitting, use U. S. 6 / 4 mm for those sections.

GAUGE
22 sts in stockinette/pattern on larger needles = 4 in / 10 cm.
Adjust needle size to obtain correct gauge if necessary.

NOTE: Read through the pattern fully before you begin to knit. There are several places where some steps occur simultaneously. Mark each occurrence of "*at the same time*" so you will be aware of these simultaneous steps.

BODY

The body is worked in the round from the bottom up. With smaller circular and Color 5, CO 220 (240, 256, 272, 296) sts. Join, being careful not to twist cast-on row; pm for beginning of rnd. Knit 6 rnds, purl 1 rnd. Change to Color 3, knit rnd, purl 1 rnd. Change to Color 4, knit 1 rnd, purl 1 rnd. Change to Color 2, knit 1 rnd, purl 1 rnd. Change to Color 1, knit 1 rnd, purl 1 rnd. Change to larger circular for single-color knitting and continue in stockinette with Color 1. Pm at each side with 110 (120, 128, 136, 148) sts each for front and back. Knit around until body measures 14¼ in / 36 cm.

Shape Armholes: BO 14 (14, 14, 14, 16) sts at each side as follow: BO 7 (7, 7, 7, 8) sts, knit until 7 (7, 7, 7, 8) sts before next marker, BO 14 (14, 14, 14, 16) sts, knit until 7 (7, 7, 7, 8) sts rem and BO 7 (7, 7, 7, 8) sts. Set body aside while you knit sleeves.

SLEEVES

The sleeves are knitted in the round. With smaller dpn and Color 5, CO 48 (48, 52, 52, 56) sts. Divide sts onto dpn and join Knit 6 rnds, purl 1 rnd. Change to Color 3, knit rnd, purl 1 rnd. Change to Color 4, knit 1 rnd, purl 1 rnd. Change to Color 2, knit 1 rnd, purl 1 rnd. Change to Color 1, knit 1 rnd, purl 1 rnd. On last rnd, increase 9 (11, 9, 11, 9) sts evenly spaced around = 57 (59, 61, 63, 65) sts. Change to larger dpn for single color and continue in stockinette with Color 1.

Shape Sleeve: *At the same time*, increase 2 sts at center of underarm on every 12th (10th, 8th, 8th, 7th) rnd until there are 71 (77, 85, 93, 101) sts. Continue without further shaping until sleeve is 18¼ (18¼, 18½, 18½, 19) in / 46 (46, 47, 47, 48) cm long.

Shape Armhole: BO 7 (7, 7, 7, 8) sts, knit until BO 7 (7, 7, 7, 8) sts rem and BO 7 (7, 7, 7, 8) sts. Set first sleeve aside while you knit second sleeve the same way.

JOINING BODY AND SLEEVES

Place all pieces on larger circular: front, right sleeve, back, left sleeve = 306 (338, 370, 402, 434) sts total. Pm at each intersection of body and sleeve = 4 markers.

Raglan Shaping: Knit until 2 sts before first marker, k2tog tbl, sl m, k2tog. Decrease the same way at each marker.

Decrease as est on every rnd 2 (3, 4, 6, 8) times = 290 (314, 338, 354, 370) sts rem.

Now decrease for raglan as est on every other rnd 3 (4, 6, 6, 7) times = 266 (282, 290, 306, 314) sts rem. Knit 1 rnd, decreasing 2 (6, 2, 6, 2)

CHART

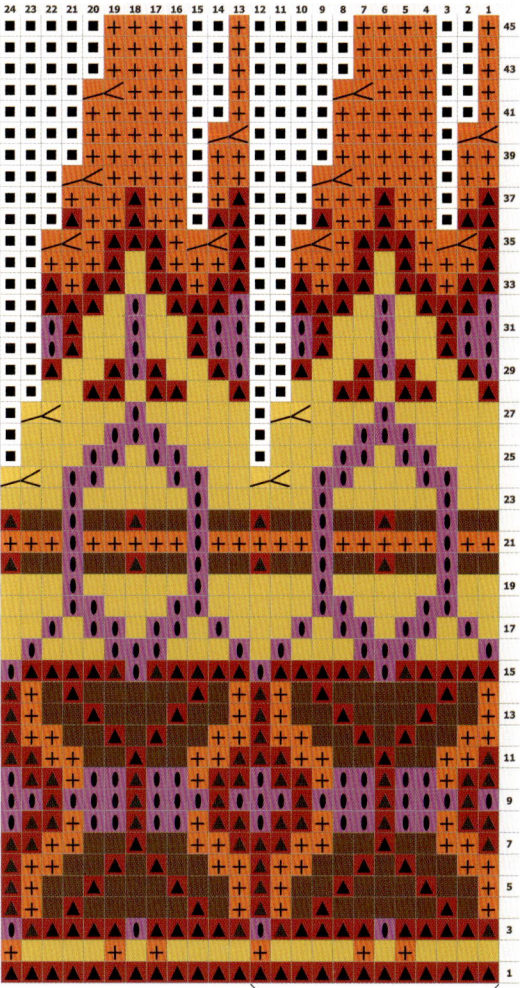

1 repeat = 12 sts

sts evenly spaced around = 264 (276, 288, 300, 312) sts rem.

Yoke Pattern: End raglan shaping—further shaping is incorporated into yoke pattern. Change to gauge-size circular for two-color knitting and work in pattern following chart, 22 (23, 24, 25, 26) rep around. Work the whole rep in length = 110 (115, 120, 125, 130) sts rem. Knit 1 rnd, decreasing 10 (11, 12, 13, 14) sts evenly spaced around = 100 (104, 108, 112, 116) sts rem. BO rem sts.

FINISHING

Weave in all ends neatly on WS. Gently steam press sweater on WS under a damp pressing cloth.

Seam underarms.
Work both rolled neckbands:
Neckband I: With U. S. 4 / 3.5 mm circular and Color 4, pick up and knit 100 (104, 108, 112, 116) sts around neck. Work 1 rnd k1tbl. Knit 8 rnds and then BO.
Neckband II: With U. S. 4 / 3.5 mm circular and Color 5, pick up and knit 100 (104, 108, 112, 116) sts around neck (behind Neckband I). Work 1 rnd k1tbl. Knit 12 rnds and then BO.
Seam underarms.

Symbols Key

■	Color 1
▨	Color 2
▨	Color 3
✚	Color 4
■	Color 5
⟋	K2tog with Color 2
⟋	K2tog with Color 4
▪	No st—the st has been decreased away

OLINE

The ribbing at the sides, topped with cables, provides this cardigan with a good fit. The soft A-line ensures that it will sit well on most bodies.

SKILL LEVEL
Easy to Intermediate

SIZES
S (M, L, XL, XXL)

FINISHED MEASUREMENTS
Chest: 34¾ (37, 39½, 39¾, 43¼, 47¼) in / 88 (94, 100, 110, 120) cm
Total Length: 24½ (26¾, 27½, 28¼, 29¼) in / 62 (68, 70, 72, 74) cm
Sleeve Length: 19 (19¼, 19¾, 20½, 20½) in / 48 (49, 0, 52, 52) cm

MATERIALS
Yarn:
CYCA #1 (fingering) Du Store Alpakka Mini Sterk (40% Merino wool, 40% alpaca, 20% polyamide, 182 yd/166 m / 50 g) **and**
CYCA #1 (light fingering) Du Store Alpakka Dreamline Air (78% Suri alpaca, 22% polyamide, 257 yd/235 m / 25 g)
NOTE: The sweater is worked with one strand of each yarn held together.
Yarn Colors and Amounts:
Color 1: Mini-Sterk: Mustard 859: 400 (450, 500, 550, 600) g
Color 2: Air: Green DL106: 150 (150, 175, 175, 200) g
Needles: U. S. size 4 / 3.5 mm: circulars and sets of 5 dpn; cable needle

GAUGE
21 sts x 29 rnds in stockinette = 4 x 4 in / 10 x 10 cm.
Adjust needle size to obtain correct gauge if necessary

Seed Stitch:
Rnd 1: *K1, p1*; rep * to * around.
Rnd 2: Work purl over knit and knit over purl.
Rep Rnd 2 for all subsequent rnds.

BODY

The sweater is worked in the round from the bottom up.

With circular and one strand of each yarn held together, CO 228 (240, 252, 272, 292) sts + 6 sts at center front for steek.

Steek: Purl steek sts; do not include steek sts in stitch counts.

Join, being careful not to twist cast-on row; pm for beginning of rnd. Knit 1 rnd, purl 1 rnd. Now work in ribbing and seed st as follows:

½ side panel on front, 20 sts: P2, (k2, p4) 3 times; pm.

Center panel on front: Work in seed st over 37 (40, 43, 48, 53) sts, p6 steek sts, and seed st over 37 (40, 43, 48, 53) sts; pm.

Side panel on front and back, 40 sts: Work (p4, k2) 6 times and end with p4; pm.

Center panel on back: Work seed st over next 74 (80, 86, 96, 106) sts; pm.

½ side panel on back, 20 sts: Work (p4, k2) 3 times, p2; pm. Work as est for 6 rnds.

On next rnd, work side panels as est, but purl the 74 (80, 86, 96, 106) center panels. Continue center panels in stockinette. When body measures a total of 7 (7½, 8, 8, 8) in / 18 (19, 20, 20, 20) cm, decrease 1 st in each purl section of side panels = 14 sts decreased around. Continue without decreasing until body measures a total of 11 (11½, 11¾, 11¾, 11¾) in / 28 (29, 30, 30, 30) cm. Decrease 1 st in each purl section of side panels = 14 sts decreased around = 200 (212, 224, 244, 264) sts rem. Work 1 rnd.

Cable Pattern: Now work cables following chart, beginning at arrow on first ½ side panel and working across chart = 13 sts. Work in stockinette to next side panel and work across chart = 26 sts. Work in stockinette to next ½ side panel and, beginning at arrow for last ½ side panel, work 13 sts of cable. Work through Row 36 of chart. Now divide body for front and back at sides between 13th and 14th sts on chart = 100 (106, 112, 122, 132) sts for back and 100 (106, 112, 122, 132) sts + 6 steek sts for front. Work each piece separately.

Back: Continue back and forth in stockinette on center panels and ribbing as on last row on chart.

Shape Armholes: BO 5 sts at each side. Then, on every other row at each side, decrease 1 st 4 times, and on every 4th row, 1 st 4 times. Continue straight up in stockinette. When armhole depth measures 8¼ (8¾, 9, 9¾, 10¾) in / 21 (22, 23, 25, 27) cm, shape back neck and shoulders *at the same time.*

Back Neck: BO the center 32 (34, 36, 38, 40) sts on back. Work each side separately. At neck edge, on every other row, BO 2 sts 2 times.

Shape Shoulder: From outer edge of shoulder, on every other row, BO 5-6-6 (6-6-7, 7-7-7, 8-8-9, 9-10-10) sts. No sts rem. Work opposite side to correspond.

Front: Work as for back, but shape V-neck at same time as shaping armholes.

V-Neck: BO 1 st along steek as follows: Work until 2 sts rem before the 6 steek sts, k2tog, p6 for steek, k2tog tbl and work as est to end of row. Decrease the same way on every RS row 20 (21, 22, 23, 24) times; 17 (19, 21, 25, 29) sts rem for shoulder. Shape shoulder as for back when 1¼ in 3 cm before total length. No sts rem. Work opposite side to correspond.

SLEEVES

With dpn and one strand of each yarn held together, CO 44 (46, 48, 52, 56) sts. Divide sts onto dpn and join. Knit 1 rnd, purl 1 rnd. Work cables and seed st as follows: Work 15 (16, 17, 19, 21) seed sts, work first 14 sts = center sts, and 15 (16, 17, 19, 21) seed sts. Work 6 more rnds as est. Purl 1 rnd and then stockinette over the 15 (16, 17, 19, 21) side sts on each side of center st instead of seed st. Begin increasing to shape sleeve, and work pattern following cable chart centered on sleeve all the way up with stockinette on each side.

Shape Sleeve: On every 5th rnd, increase 2 sts centered on underarm until there are 80 (84, 88, 96, 100) sts. Work new sts in stockinette. Continue without further increases until sleeve is 19 (19¼, 19¾, 20½, 20½) in / 48 (49, 50, 52, 52) cm long.

Sleeve Cap: Divide sleeve at center of underarm and work back and forth. BO 5 sts on each side of sleeve and then, on every other row, BO 2 sts once and 1 st 4 (4, 5, 6, 6) times. Work 3 rows and then, on every 4th row, BO 1 st 3 times. BO 4 sts at beginning of each of next 10 rows. BO rem sts. Make second sleeve the same way.

FINISHING

Weave in all ends neatly on WS. *Gently* steam press sweater on WS under a damp pressing cloth. Machine-stitch 2 lines, zigzag and straight stitch, on each side of center front sts. Carefully cut open up center of steek.

Join shoulders.

Front Bands and Collar: With circular and one strand of each yarn

CHART

26 25 24 23 22 21 20 19 18 17 16 15 14 13 12 11 10 9 8 7 6 5 4 3 2 1

1 repeat in length

14 center sts on sleeve
14 center sts on band/collar

Begin here for first ½ side panel, all sizes

Begin here for 2nd side panel, and on last ½ side panel, all sizes

Symbols Key

	Knit on RS, purl on WS
•	Purl on WS, knit on RS
⟋⟍	Place 2 sts on cable needle and hold in front of work, p1, k2 from cable needle
⟋⟍	Place 1 st on cable needle and hold in back of work, k2, p1 from cable needle
⟋⟍	Place 3 sts on cable needle and hold in front of work, k3, k3 from cable needle

held together, CO 34 sts. P4, k2 = edge sts. Pm and work (p4, k2) 3 times, p4 = center of band/collar. Pm and (k2, p4) = edge sts. Continue as est until piece measures 7 (7½, 8, 8, 8) in / 18 (19, 20, 20, 20) cm. Decrease 1 st in each purl section of center sts = 4 sts decreased.

NOTE: Do not decrease in edge sts. Work straight up until piece measures 11 (11½, 11¾, 11¾, 11¾) in / 28 (29, 30, 30, 30) cm. Decrease 1 st in each purl section of center st = 4 sts decreased and 26 sts rem. Work cable pattern following chart over the 14 center sts for 1 rep in length. On next row, increase 1 st in each purl section of center sts = 4 sts increased. Work in ribbing for 4 in / 10 cm and then increase 1 st in each purl section of center sts = 4 sts increased and there are 34 sts. Continue until band/collar, when lightly stretched, reaches center of back neck. Work the other half of the band/collar in reverse: increase where you previously decreased and decrease where you previously increased. BO.

Sew band/collar with back stitch to fronts and neck with RS facing RS. Sew so the outermost 4 purl sts form a facing folded over cut edges of steek. Sew facing down smoothly. Attach sleeves.

TUMI

"Tumi" is a Scandinavian name with its origins in Old Norse; it means "happiness" and "courage." I don't know whether this sweater will give you courage, but perhaps it can make you happy! Tumi is super light and soft, so you're bound to love it. The pullover has raglan shaping and a gorgeous wave pattern reminiscent of Viking ships on a sea expedition. For a cardigan with the same pattern, see Myra on page 40.

SKILL LEVEL
Easy to Intermediate

SIZES
S (M, L, XL, XXL)

FINISHED MEASUREMENTS
Chest: 35½ (38½, 41¼, 44, 50) in / 90 (98, 105, 112, 127) cm
Total Length: 24 (24¾, 25½, 26½, 27¼) in / 61 (63, 65, 67, 69) cm
Sleeve Length: 18½ (19, 19, 19¼, 19¼) in / 47 (48, 48, 49, 49) cm

MATERIALS
Yarn:
CYCA #1 (light fingering) Naturally Yarns New Zealand Amuri 4-ply (75% Merino wool, 25% possum, 262 yd/240 m / 50 g)
Yarn Colors and Amounts:
Green Heather 4025: 250 (250, 300, 350, 400) g
Needles: U. S. size 4 / 3.5 mm circulars and sets of 5 dpn

GAUGE
24 sts in ribbing = 4 in / 10 cm.
Adjust needle size to obtain correct gauge if necessary.

BODY

The body is worked in the round from the bottom up.
With circular, CO 217 (235, 253, 271, 307) sts. Join, being careful not to twist cast-on row; pm for beginning of rnd. Knit 1 rnd, purl 1 rnd, knit 1 rnd, purl 1 rnd. Work pattern following chart: Begin with first 18 sts on chart, work 18-st repeat 11 (12, 13, 14, 16) times, and end with last st on chart. Work 1 rep in length, but on Rnd 42, k2tog with first and last sts of rnd = 216 (234, 252, 270, 306) sts.

Dividing for front and back: Pm so you have p1, k3, p1 at center front, with beginning of rnd as close to side as possible. Cut yarn and pm at each side = 108 (117, 126, 135, 153) sts each for front and back. Beginning at front, work around, repeating Rows 43-44 of chart for remainder of piece, until body measures 15¾ (16¼, 16½, 16½, 17) in / 40 (41, 42, 42, 43) cm.

Shape Armholes: BO 8 sts on each side as follows: BO 4 sts, work until 4 sts before next side marker, BO 8 sts, work until 4 sts before side marker and BO 4.

SLEEVES

The sleeves are worked in the round. With dpn, CO 55 (55, 55, 55, 73) sts. Divide sts onto dpn and join. Knit 1 rnd, purl 1 rnd, knit 1 rnd, purl 1 rnd. Work pattern following chart: Begin with first 18 sts on chart, work 18-st repeat 2 (2, 2, 2, 3) times, and end with last st on chart. Work Rows 15-44 of chart and then rep Rows 43-44 for rest of sleeve.

At the same time;
Shape Sleeve: Increase 2 sts centered on underarm every 6th rnd from start of sleeve until there are

Symbols Key

⁄	K2tog
•	Purl
☐	Knit
ƍ	Yo
ʌ	Sl 1, k2tog, psso
⋋	K2tog tbl

87 (91, 97, 103, 113) sts. Continue without further shaping until sleeve is 18½ (19, 19, 19¼, 19¼) in / 47 (48, 48, 49, 49) cm long.
Shape Armhole: BO 4 sts, work until 4 sts rem, BO 4 sts.
Set first sleeve aside while you knit second sleeve the same way.

JOINING BODY AND SLEEVES

Place all pieces on circular: front, right sleeve, back, left sleeve = 358 (384, 414, 444, 498) sts total. Pm at each intersection of body and sleeve = 4 markers. Work 2 rnds without decreasing.
Raglan Shaping: Knit until 2 sts before first marker, k2tog tbl, sl m, k2tog. Decrease the same way at each marker.
Decrease as est on every rnd 4 (5, 6, 7, 9) times = 326 (344, 366, 388, 426) sts rem.
Now decrease for raglan as est on every other rnd 25 (26, 28, 29, 33) times.
At the same time, when 7 raglan decrease rnds rem and 182 (192, 198, 212, 218) sts rem, BO the center 30 (32, 34, 36, 38) sts for front neck. Now work back and forth. On each side of neck, on every other row, BO 2 sts 2 times and 1 st 2 (2, 3, 3, 3) times.

CHART

NOTES REGARDING CHART: The pattern moves sideways by working 3tog and making 2 yarnovers on each repeat. Therefore, on the chart, the knit and purl sts are not always worked over each other, as drawn in. Work each round/row as shown so the pattern will work out correctly.

Continue with raglan shaping on every RS row until all decreases have been worked. BO rem sts.
Neckband: With circular, pick up and knit 72 (74, 76, 78, 80) sts along front neck and 60 (62, 64, 66, 68) sts along back. Work 1 rnd k1tbl and then purl 1 rnd, knit 1 rnd, purl 1 rnd, knit 1 rnd, purl 1 rnd, knit 5 rnds. BO.

FINISHING

Weave in all ends neatly on WS. *Gently* steam press sweater on WS under a damp pressing cloth. Seam underarms.

QUEEN OF DIAMONDS

A popular sweater named for the queen of the card deck. The pullover has raglan shaping, long ribbing on the body and sleeves, and a loose-fitting high neck. It's perfect for when you're on the job, and cozy on cold days.

SKILL LEVEL
Intermediate

SIZES
S (M, L, XL, XXL)

FINISHED MEASUREMENTS
Chest: 34¾ (37, 39½, 44, 48¾) in / 88 (94, 100, 112, 124) cm
Total Length: 22¾ (23¾, 23¾, 24½, 25¼) in / 58 (60, 60, 62, 64) cm
Sleeve Length: approx. 19¾ (19¾, 19¾, 19¾, 19¾) in / 50 (50, 50, 50, 50) cm

MATERIALS
Yarn:
CYCA #3 (DK, light worsted) Rowan Felted Tweed (50% Merino wool, 25% alpaca, 25% viscose, 191 yd/175 m / 50 g)
Yarn Colors and Amounts:
Color 1: Clay 177: 150 (150, 200, 200, 250) g
Color 2: Pine 158: 50 (50, 50, 50, 100) g
Color 3: Watery 152: 50 (50, 100, 100, 100) g
Color 4: Avocado 161: 50 (50, 100, 100, 100) g
Color 5: Mineral 181: 150 (150, 200, 200, 250) g
Needles: U. S. sizes 2.5 and 4 / 3 and 3.5 mm: circulars and sets of 5 dpn. If you work two-color stranded knitting more tightly than one-color knitting, use U. S. 6 / 4 mm for those sections.

GAUGE
22 sts in stockinette/pattern on larger needles = 4 in / 10 cm.
Adjust needle size to obtain correct gauge if necessary.

BODY

The body is worked in the round from the bottom up. With smaller circular and Color 5, CO 192 (208, 220, 244, 268) sts. Join, being careful not to twist cast-on row; pm for beginning of rnd. Work around in k2tbl, p2 ribbing for 6 in / 15 cm. Change to larger circular for two-color knitting and knit 1 rnd, *at the same time* adjusting stitch count to 192 (210, 222, 246, 270). Work in pattern following chart, beginning at arrow. When body measures 14¼ (14½, 14½, 15, 15¾) in / 36 (37, 37, 38, 40) cm, pm at each side with 96 (105, 111, 123, 135) sts each for front and back. Pm on pattern rnd where you ended.

Shape Armholes: BO 8 sts on each side as follows: BO 4 sts, knit until 4 sts before next side marker, BO 8 sts, knit until 4 sts before side marker and BO 4.

SLEEVES

The sleeves are worked in the round. With smaller dpn and Color 5, CO 52 (56, 56, 60, 60) sts. Divide sts onto dpn and join. Work around in k2tbl, p2 ribbing for 5½ in / 14 cm. Change to larger dpn for two-color knitting and knit 1 rnd, *at the same time* increasing 8 (7, 9, 9, 11) sts evenly spaced around = 60 (63, 65, 69, 71) sts. Work pattern following the chart. See arrow for center of sleeve and count back to determine first st of rnd. *At the same time:*

Shape Sleeve: Increase 2 sts centered on underarm every 8th rnd until there are 75 (81, 91, 97, 107) sts. Continue without further shaping until sleeve is approx. 19¾ in / 50 cm long (all sizes). Make sure you end on same round as for body.

Shape Armhole: BO 4 sts, knit until 4 sts rem, BO 4 sts.
Set first sleeve aside while you knit second sleeve the same way.

JOINING BODY AND SLEEVES

Place all pieces on circular of size needed to obtain gauge for two-color knitting: front, right sleeve, back, left sleeve = 310 (340, 372, 408, 452) sts total. Pm at each intersection of body and sleeve = 4 markers. Continue in pattern as est. Work 2 rnds without decreasing.

Raglan Shaping: Knit until 2 sts before first marker, k2tog tbl, sl m, k2tog. Decrease the same way at each marker.

Decrease as est on every rnd 2 (3, 5, 6, 7) times = 294 (316, 332, 360, 396) sts rem.

Now decrease for raglan as est on every other rnd a total of 25 (26, 27, 29, 33) times.

At the same time, when 6 raglan decrease rnds rem and 142 (156, 164, 176, 180) sts rem, BO the center front 22 (23, 25, 27, 27) sts for front neck.

Now work back and forth. On each side of neck, on every other row, BO 2 sts 2 times and 1 st 2 (2, 3, 3, 3) times.

Continue with raglan shaping on every RS row until all decreases have been worked. BO rem sts.

FINISHING

Weave in all ends neatly on WS. *Gently* steam press sweater on WS under a damp pressing cloth. Seam underarms.

Neckband: With larger circular for single color and Color 5, pick up and knit 108 (112, 116, 120, 124) sts around neck. Work 1 rnd k1tbl and then work in k2tbl, p2 ribbing for 2½ in / 6 cm. Turn work and work on WS, continuing ribbing for a total of 7 in / 18 cm. BO in ribbing. Fold neckband forward.

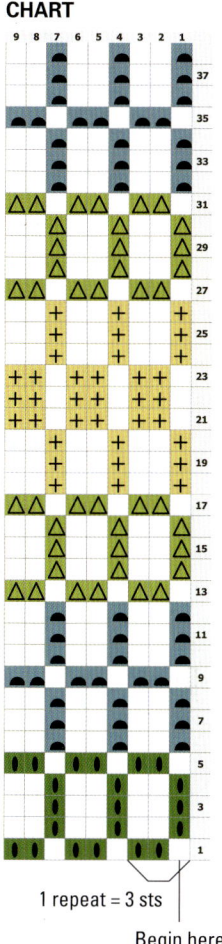

CHART

1 repeat = 3 sts

Begin here

Symbols Key

☐ Color 1
■ Color 2
◼ Color 3
△ Color 4
+ Color 5

SUNFLOWER

A sweater name to put you into a sunshiny mood. The Sunflower pullover is roomy, with a round yoke, wide neck, and narrow ribbed bands.

SKILL LEVEL
Intermediate

SIZES
S (M, L, XL, XXL)

FINISHED MEASUREMENTS
Chest: 44 (47¼, 49¾, 53½, 57½) in / 112 (120, 126, 136, 146) cm
Total Length: 21¼ (21¾, 22, 22¾, 23¾) in / 54 (55, 56, 58, 60) cm
The sweater is wide and short. You can adjust the length as you prefer.
Sleeve Length: 18¼ (18¼, 18½, 18½, 19) in / 46 (46, 47, 47, 48) cm

MATERIALS
Yarn:
CYCA #2 (sport, baby) Hillesvåg Ask/Hifa 2 (100% Norwegian wool, 344 yd/315 m / 100 g)
Yarn Colors and Amounts:
Color 1: Sun-Yellow 6118: 300 (350, 350, 400, 450) g
Color 2: Ecru 6107: 50 (50, 100, 100, 100) g
Color 3: Lime-Green 6113: 50 (50, 50, 50, 50) g
Color 4: Light Lime 6120: 50 (50, 50, 50, 50) g
Color 5: Golden-Brown 6093: 50 (50, 50, 50, 50) g
Needles: U. S. sizes 1.5 and 2.5 / 2.5 and 3 mm: circulars and sets of 5 dpn. If you work two-color stranded knitting more tightly than one-color knitting, use U. S. 4 / 3.5 mm for those sections.

GAUGE
24 sts in stockinette/pattern on larger needles = 4 in / 10 cm.
Adjust needle size to obtain correct gauge if necessary.

CHART

Symbols Key

- ■ Color 1
- ☐ Color 2
- ◆ Color 3
- + Color 4
- ▨ Color 5
- ⧄ K2tog with Color 1
- ⧅ K2tog with Color 2
- ⧄ K2tog with Color 4
- ■ No stitch—st has been decreased away

1 repeat = 12 sts

BODY

The body is worked in the round from the bottom up. With larger circular and Color 1, CO 268 (288, 304, 324, 352) sts. Join, being careful not to twist cast-on row; pm for beginning of rnd. Work around in k2, p2 ribbing for 9 rnds. Continue in stockinette until body measures 12¼ in / 31 cm. Pm at each side with 134 (144, 152, 162, 176) sts each for front and back.

Shape Armholes: BO 12 (12, 12, 12, 14) sts on each side as follows: BO 6 (6, 6, 6, 7) sts, knit until 6 (6, 6, 6, 7) sts before next side marker, BO 12 (12, 12, 12, 14) sts, knit until 6 (6, 6, 6, 7) sts before side marker and BO 6 (6, 6, 6, 7) sts. Set body aside while you knit sleeves.

SLEEVES

The sleeves are worked in the round. With smaller dpn and Color 1, CO 52 (52, 56, 56, 60) sts. Divide sts onto dpn and join. Work around in k2, p2 ribbing for 9 rnds. Change to larger dpn for single color and knit 1 rnd, at the same time increasing 1 in every 4th st = 13 (13, 14, 14, 15) sts increased.

Sizes S, M, and XXL: Increase 1 extra st = 66 (66, 70, 70, 76) sts Continue in stockinette, and *at the same time* shape sleeve:

Shape Sleeve: Increase 2 sts centered on underarm every 12th rnd until there are 80 (88, 96, 104, 116) sts. Continue without further shaping until sleeve is approx. 18¼ (18¼, 18½, 18½, 19) in / 46 (46, 47, 47, 48) cm long.

Shape Armhole: BO 6 (6, 6, 6, 7) sts, knit until 6 (6, 6, 6, 7) sts rem, BO 6 (6, 6, 6, 7) sts.

Set first sleeve aside while you knit second sleeve the same way.

JOINING BODY AND SLEEVES

Place all pieces on circular of size needed to obtain gauge in one-color knitting: front, right sleeve, back, left sleeve = 380 (416, 448, 484, 528) sts total. Pm at each intersection of body and sleeve = 4 markers. Work 2 rnds without decreasing.

Raglan Shaping: Knit until 2 sts before first marker, k2tog tbl, sl m, k2tog. Decrease the same way at each marker.

Decrease as est on every rnd 2 (4, 5, 5, 8) times = 364 (384, 408, 444, 464) sts rem.

Now decrease for raglan as est on every other rnd 3 (3, 4, 4, 5) times = 340 (360, 376, 412, 424) sts rem. Knit 1 rnd, decreasing 4 (0, 4, 4, 4) sts evenly spaced around = 336 (360, 372, 408, 420) sts rem.

Yoke Pattern: End raglan shaping—further shaping is incorporated into yoke pattern. Change to circular of size needed to obtain gauge for two-color knitting and work in pattern following chart, 28 (30, 31, 34, 35) rep around. Work the whole rep in length = 112 (120, 124, 136, 140) sts rem. BO rem sts.

FINISHING

Neckband: With smaller circular and Color 1, pick up and knit 1 st in each st around neck = 112 (120, 124, 136, 140) sts around neck. Work 1 rnd k1tbl and then work in k2tbl, p2 ribbing for 9 rnds. BO in ribbing. *Gently* steam press sweater on WS under a damp pressing cloth. Seam underarms.

KLARA

The colorful Klara cardigan is one of my most popular designs. This sweater has a round neck with heart motifs in fresh colors, and crocheted front bands. The suggested yarn comes in more than a hundred colors, so you can play with them and make your own completely special Klara cardigan.

SKILL LEVEL
Intermediate to Experienced

SIZES
S (M, L, XL, XXL)

FINISHED MEASUREMENTS
Chest: 35½ (38½, 41¾, 48¾, 54¼) in / 90 (98, 106, 124, 138) cm
Total Length: 24½ (24¾, 25¼, 26, 26¾) in / 62 (63, 64, 66, 68) cm
Sleeve Length: 19 (19, 19¼, 19¼, 19¼) in / 48 (48, 49, 49, 49) cm

MATERIALS
Yarn:
CYCA #2 (sport, baby) Hillesvåg Ask/Hifa 2 (100% Norwegian wool, 344 yd/315 m / 100 g)

Yarn Colors and Amounts:
Color 1: Light Green Turquoise Heather 6584: 300 (300, 350, 350, 400) g
Color 2: Peasant Blue 6082: 50 (50, 100, 100, 100) g
Color 3: Bright Apple-Green Heather 6588: 50 (50, 50, 50, 50) g
Color 4: Purple Heather 6577: 50 (50, 50, 50, 50) g
Color 5: Cognac 6095: 50 (50, 50, 50, 50) g
Color 6: Red-Brown 6009: 50 (50, 50, 50, 50) g
Needles: U. S. sizes 1.5 and 2.5 / 2.5 and 3 mm: circulars and sets of 5 dpn. If you work two-color stranded knitting more tightly than one-color knitting, use U. S. 4 / 3.5 mm for those sections.
Crochet Hook: U. S. size B-1 or C-2 / 2.5 mm
Notions: 10 buttons to match colors of cardigan; approx. 1.6 yd / 1.5 m ribbon to cover cut edges of seek

GAUGE
24 sts in stockinette/pattern on larger needles = 4 in / 10 cm.
Adjust needle size to obtain correct gauge if necessary.

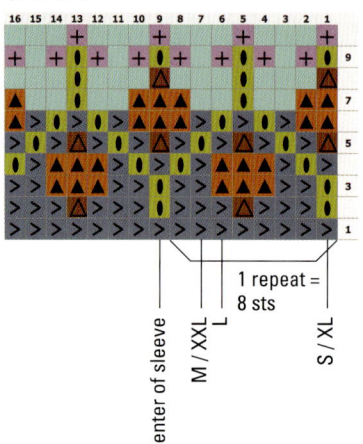

CHART I

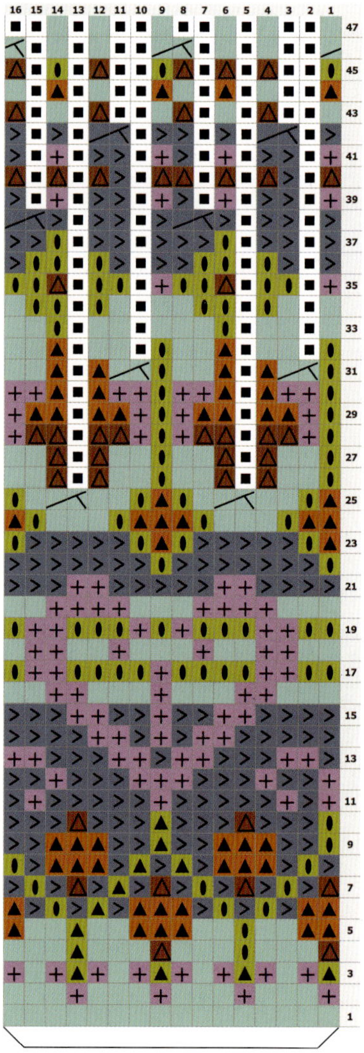

1 repeat = 16 sts

CHART II

1 repeat = 8 sts

Center of sleeve
M / XXL
L
S / XL

Symbols Key

- ▢ Color 1
- ▶ Color 2
- ▮ Color 3
- + Color 4
- ▲ Color 5
- ⬟ Color 6
- ⟋ K2tog with Color 1
- ⟍ K2tog with Color 2
- ■ No stitch—st has been decreased away

BODY

The sweater is worked in the round from the bottom up.

With smaller circular and Color 2, CO 217 (235, 255, 297, 331) sts + 6 sts at center front for steek.

Steek: Purl steek sts; do not include steek sts in stitch counts. To make cutting and sewing later easier, and to secure the yarns, work the 2 center sts with pattern color.

Knit 1 row and turn. Join, being careful not to twist cast-on row; pm for beginning of rnd.

Ribbing: Work 6 rnds ribbing as follows: K2 (3, 1, 2, 3) tbl, *p1, k3tbl*; rep from * to * until 3 (0, 2, 3, 0) sts rem, p1 (0, 1, 1, 0), k2 (0, 1, 2, 0) tbl. Change to larger circular (size needed to obtain gauge for two-color knitting) and work in pattern following Chart II. Begin at arrow for your size and work around in pattern for 1 rep in length. Continue in stockinette with Color 1 and larger circular (size needed to obtain gauge for one-color knitting). Work until body measures 15½ in / 39 cm (all sizes). Pm at each side with 54 (58, 63, 73, 82) sts for each front (make sure the 6 steek sts are at center front) and 109 (119, 129, 151, 167) sts for back.

Shape Armholes: BO 12 (12, 12, 12, 14) sts on each side as follows: BO 6 (6, 6, 6, 7) sts, knit until 6 (6, 6, 6, 7) sts before next side marker, BO 12 (12, 12, 12, 14) sts, knit until 6 (6, 6, 6, 7) sts before next side marker and BO 12 (12, 12, 12, 14) sts, knit until 6 (6, 6, 6, 7) sts rem, BO 6 (6, 6, 6, 7) sts. Set body aside while you knit sleeves.

SLEEVES

Read through this section fully before you begin knitting to make sure you are aware of all simultaneous steps.

With smaller dpn and Color 2, CO 52 (52, 56, 60, 64) sts. Divide sts onto dpn and join. Work 8 rnds k3tbl, p1 ribbing.

Change to larger dpn (size needed to obtain gauge for two-color knitting) and work in pattern following Chart II, with 1 rep in length. See arrow for center of sleeve and count back to determine first st of rnd. After completing pattern, continue in stockinette with Color 1 and larger dpn (size needed to obtain gauge for one-color knitting).

At the same time:

Shape Sleeve: On every 8th rnd, increase 2 sts centered on underarm until there are 80 (88, 96, 104, 116) sts. Continue without further increases until sleeve is 19 (19, 19¼, 19¼, 19¼) in / 48 (48, 49, 49, 49) cm long.

Shape Armhole: BO 6 (6, 6, 6, 7) sts, knit until 6 (6, 6, 6, 7) sts rem, BO 6 (6, 6, 6, 7) sts. Set first sleeve aside while you knit second sleeve the same way.

JOINING BODY AND SLEEVES

Place all pieces on circular (size needed to obtain gauge for one-color knitting): front, right sleeve, back, left sleeve = 329 (363, 399, 457, 507) sts total. Pm at each intersection of body and sleeve = 4 markers. Knit 1 rnd with Color 1, decreasing 8 (10, 7, 8, 10) sts evenly spaced around (but not in steek) = 321 (353, 392, 449, 497) sts rem.

Raglan Shaping: Knit until 2 sts before first marker, k2tog tbl, sl m, k2tog. Decrease the same way at each marker.

Decrease as est on every rnd 2 (4, 5, 6, 8) times = 305 (321, 352, 401, 433) sts rem.

Yoke Pattern: End raglan shaping—further shaping is incorporated into yoke pattern. Change to circular of size needed to obtain gauge for two-color knitting, and work in pattern following Chart I, 19 (20, 22, 25, 27) rep around + 1st on chart, so pattern will be symmetrical at center front. Work the whole rep in length = 115 (121, 132, 151, 163) sts rem. BO rem sts.

FINISHING

Weave in all ends neatly on WS. Gently steam press sweater on WS under a damp pressing cloth. Machine-stitch 2 lines, zigzag and straight stitch, on each side of center front sts. Carefully cut open up center of steek.

Seam underarms.

Front and Neck Bands: Begin at lower right front, with crochet hook and Color 2.

Work in sc up right front (fold steek to WS and work sc on foldline), 2 sc in corner and then sc along neck, 2 sc in corner, and sc down left front. Turn, change to Color 6 and work 1 row of sc back.

Buttonhole Row: Mark spacing for 10 buttonholes, evenly spaced down right front band. Turn and work 1 row sc with Color 5, *at the same time* making buttonholes: Ch 4, skip 3 sc, 2 sc in next sc. After working buttonhole row, turn and, with Color 3, work 1 row sc, with 3 sc in each ch-4 loop. Turn and change to Color 4 and work 1 row sc.

Turn and change to Color 1 and work 1 row sc. Cut yarn and fasten off.

Sew buttons onto left band spaced as for buttonholes. Sew ribbon to cover cut steek edges.

VANDA

This delicate cardigan is patterned and has long ribbing for the sleeve cuffs. Distinguishing features include a round yoke in retro-inspired colors, crocheted bands, and a folded hem at the lower edge.

SKILL LEVEL
Intermediate to Experienced

SIZES
S (M, L, XL, XXL)

FINISHED MEASUREMENTS
Chest: 34¾ (37, 39½, 44, 48¾) in / 88 (94, 100, 112, 124) cm
Total Length: 22¾ (23¼, 23¾, 24½, 25¼) in / 58 (59, 60, 62, 64) cm
Sleeve Length: approx. 19 (19, 19¼, 19¼, 19¼) in / 48 (48, 49, 49, 49) cm

MATERIALS
Yarn:
CYCA #2 (sport, baby) Hillesvåg Ask/Hifa 2 (100% Norwegian wool, 344 yd/315 m / 100 g)

Yarn Colors and Amounts:
Color 1: Light Green-Turquoise 6127: 100 (150, 150, 150, 200) g
Color 2: Mint Green Heather 6587: 250 (300, 300, 350, 350) g
Color 3: Ecru 6107: 50 (50, 50, 50, 50) g
Color 4: Beige 6142: 50 (50, 50, 50, 50) g
Needles: U. S. sizes 1.5 and 2.5 / 2.5 and 3 mm: circulars and sets of 5 dpn. If you work two-color stranded knitting more tightly than one-color knitting, use U. S. 4 / 3.5 mm for those sections.
Crochet Hook: U. S. size B-1 or C-2 / 2.5 mm
Notions: 5 buttons you think will be pretty on the sweater; approx. 1.6 yd / 1.5 m pretty ribbon to cover cut edges of seek

GAUGE
24 sts in stockinette/pattern on larger needles = 4 in / 10 cm.
Adjust needle size to obtain correct gauge if necessary.

BODY

The sweater is worked in the round from the bottom up.

With smaller circular and Color 1, CO 211 (225, 241, 269, 297) sts + 6 sts at center front for steek.

Steek: Purl steek sts; do not include steek sts in stitch counts. To make cutting and sewing later easier, and to secure the yarns, work the 3 center sts with pattern color.

Join, being careful not to twist cast-on row; pm for beginning of rnd. Knit 7 rnds and then purl 1 rnd for foldline. Change to Color 2 and knit 7 rnds. Change to larger circular for single color and continue in stockinette until body above foldline measures 13¾ in / 35 cm.

Pm at each side, with 52 (55, 59, 66, 73) sts for each front (make sure the 6 steek sts are at center front), and 107 (115, 123, 137, 151) sts for back.

Shape Armholes: BO 12 (12, 12, 12, 14) sts on each side as follows: Knit until 6 (6, 6, 6, 7) sts before first side marker, BO 12 (12, 12, 12, 14) sts, knit until 6 (6, 6, 6, 7) sts before next side marker, BO 12 (12, 12, 12, 14) sts, knit to end of rnd. Set body aside while you knit sleeves.

SLEEVES

Read through this section fully before you begin knitting to make sure you are aware of all simultaneous steps.

The sleeves are worked in the round. With smaller dpn and Color 1, CO 56 (56, 60, 60, 64) sts. Divide sts onto dpn and join. Work in k2 tbl, p2 ribbing for 4¾ in / 12 cm. Knit 1 rnd, increasing 3 (5, 3, 5, 3) sts evenly spaced around = 59 (61, 63, 65, 67) sts. Change to larger dpn (size needed to obtain gauge for two-color knitting) and work in pattern following Chart II. See arrow for center of sleeve and count back to determine first st of rnd. Work 1 rep of chart in length. Change to dpn of size needed to obtain gauge for one-color knitting and continue in Color 2 for rest of sleeve.

At the same time:

Shape Sleeve: On every 8th rnd from start of sleeve, increase 2 sts centered on underarm until there are 79 (89, 95, 101, 113) sts.

After completing pattern, continue in stockinette for rest of sleeve with Color 2 and larger dpn (size needed to obtain gauge for one-color knitting).

Continue without further increases until sleeve is 19 (19, 19¼, 19¼, 19¼) in / 48 (48, 49, 49, 49) cm long.

Shape Armhole: BO 6 (6, 6, 6, 7) sts, knit until 6 (6, 6, 6, 7) sts rem, BO 6 (6, 6, 6, 7) sts. Set first sleeve aside while you knit second sleeve the same way.

JOINING BODY AND SLEEVES

Place all pieces on circular (size needed to obtain gauge for one-color knitting): front, right sleeve, back, left sleeve = 321 (355, 383, 423, 467) sts total. Pm at each intersection of body and sleeve = 4 markers. Knit 1 rnd with Color 1, adjusting stitch count—decrease 2 (0, 0, 4, 0) sts evenly spaced around (but not in steek) = 319 (355, 383, 419, 467) sts rem.

Raglan Shaping: Knit until 2 sts before first marker, k2tog tbl, sl m, k2tog. Decrease the same way at each marker.

Decrease as est on every rnd 2 (4, 5, 7, 8) times = 303 (323, 343, 363, 403) sts rem.

Yoke Pattern: End raglan shaping—further shaping is incorporated into yoke pattern. Change to circular of size needed to obtain gauge for two-color knitting, and work in pattern following Chart I. Work first 2 sts on chart, 15 (16, 17, 18, 20) rep across, and end with last st on chart. Work the whole rep in length = 93 (99, 105, 111, 123) sts rem. BO rem sts.

FINISHING

Weave in all ends neatly on WS. Gently steam press sweater on WS under a damp pressing cloth. Machine-stitch 2 lines, zigzag and straight stitch, on each side of center front sts. Carefully cut open up center of steek.

Seam underarms.

Front and Neck Bands: Begin at lower right front, with crochet hook and Color 1.

Work in sc up right front (fold steek to WS and work sc on foldline), 2 sc in corner and then sc along neck, 2 sc in corner, and sc down left front. The edging should tighten very slightly. Turn, change to Color 4, and work 1 row of sc back. Change to Color 2 and work 1 row sc. Turn, change to Color 1, and work 1 row sc.

Buttonhole Row: Mark spacing for 5 buttonholes, evenly spaced down right front band, from neck and down to beginning of pattern on yoke. With Color 1, turn and work 1 row sc, *at the same time* making buttonholes: Ch 4, skip 3 sc, 1 sc in next sc. After working buttonhole row, turn, and with Color 1, work 2 rows sc, with 3 sc in each ch-4 loop. Turn, change to Color 4, and work 1 row sc.

Turn, change to Color 2, and work 1 row sc. Cut yarn and fasten off.

CHART I

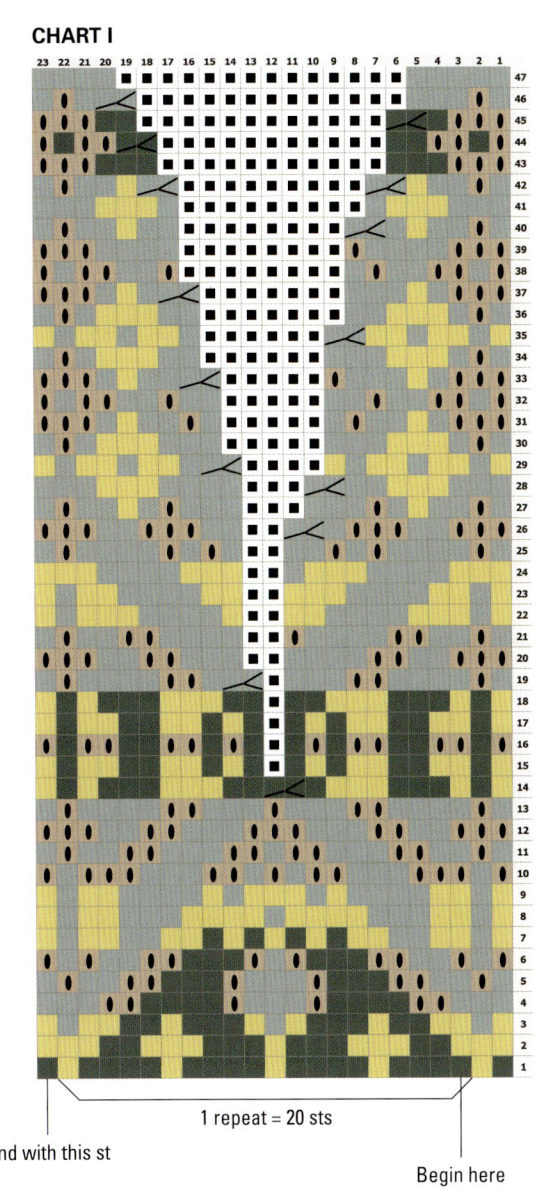

1 repeat = 20 sts

End with this st

Begin here

CHART II

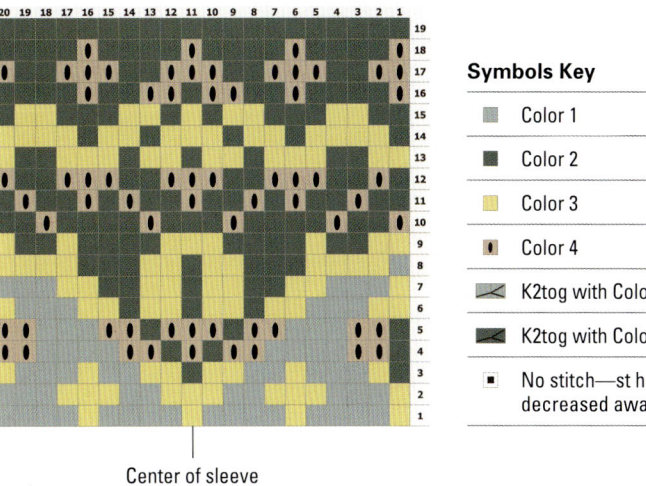

Center of sleeve

Symbols Key

- Color 1
- Color 2
- Color 3
- Color 4
- K2tog with Color 1
- K2tog with Color 2
- No stitch—st has been decreased away

Weave in all ends neatly on WS. Sew buttons onto left band spaced to match buttonholes. Sew ribbon to cover cut steek edges.

SPRING SHOOTS

This cabled pullover is knitted with two strands of the finest mohair and silk held together. The crocheted edgings in turquoise glitter yarn add little knots for effect on an otherwise classic sweater.

SKILL LEVEL
Intermediate to Experienced

SIZES
S (M, L, XL)

FINISHED MEASUREMENTS
Chest: 35½ (37, 39½, 44) in / 90 (94, 100, 112) cm
Total Length: 22¾ (23¾, 24½, 25¼) in / 58 (60, 62, 64) cm
Sleeve Length: 19 (19¼, 19¾, 20) in / 48 (49, 50, 51) cm

MATERIALS
Yarn:
CYCA #0 (lace) Rowan Kidsilk Haze (70% mohair, 30% silk, 299 yd/209 m / 25 g)
and
CYCA #1 (fingering) Rauma Concorde (64% rayon, 36% polyester, 137 yd/125 m / 25 g)
Yarn Colors and Amounts:
Color 1: Kidsilk Haze: Grass Green 597: 300 (325, 350, 375) g
Color 2: Concorde: Dark Blue 23: 50 (50, 50, 50) g
The sweater is worked with doubled yarn.
Needles: U. S. sizes 4 and 6 / 3.5 and 4 mm circulars and sets of 5 dpn; cable needle
Crochet Hook: U. S. E-4 / 3.5 mm

GAUGE
30 sts in cable pattern with doubled Kidsilk Haze on larger needles = 4 in / 10 cm.
Adjust needle size to obtain correct gauge if necessary.

BODY

The sweater is worked in the round from the bottom up. With two strands of Color 1 (Kidsilk Haze) held together and larger circular, CO 270 (282, 299, 334) sts. Knit 1 row = WS. Now join, being careful not to twist; pm for beginning of rnd. Work 0 (k1tbl, p1, k1tbl; k1tbl, p1, k1tbl, p1, k1tbl, p1, k1tbl; p1, k1tbl, p1, k1tbl). Work 4 (4, 4, 5) cables following Chart I = 48 (48, 48, 60) sts, then cables following Chart II = 39 sts, then 4 (4, 4, 5) cables following Chart III = 48 (48, 48, 60) sts, ending with 0 (k1tbl, p1, k1tbl; k1bl, p1, k1tbl, p1, k1tbl, p1, k1tbl; p1, k1tbl, p1, k1tbl) = front. Pm at side and work back as for front until body measures a total of 12¾ (13, 13½, 13½) in / 32 (33, 34, 34) cm. Divide work at side markers = 135 (141, 149, 167) sts each for front and back. Now work each side separately.

Front: BO 6 sts at each side for armholes. Next, at each side at beginning of every row, decrease 1 st 5 times = 113 (119, 127, 145) sts rem. Work without further decreasing in pattern as est until 3¼ in / 8 cm before total length.

Shape Neck: BO center 25 (27, 29, 31) sts for front neck. Work each side separately. At neck edge, on every other row, BO 2 sts 3 times and 1 st 6 times.

At the same time, 1¼ in / 3 cm before total length, shape shoulder: from outer edge of shoulder, on every other row, BO 10-11-11 (11-11-12, 12-12-13, 15-15-15) sts.

Work other side the same way, reversing shaping to correspond.

Back: Work as for front until 1¼ in / 3 cm before total length.

Shape Back Neck and Shoulders: BO center 43 (45, 47, 49) sts for back neck. Work each side separately. At neck edge, on every other row, BO 2 sts 1 time and 1 st 1 time. Work other side the same way, reversing shaping to correspond. *At the same time*, shape shoulders as for front until no sts rem at shoulders.

SLEEVES

The sleeves are worked in the round. With two strands of Color 1 (Kidsilk Haze) held together and smaller dpn, CO 50 (52, 54, 56) sts. Divide sts onto dpn and join. Knit 6 rnds, purl 1 rnd. Change to larger dpn and knit 1 rnd, at the same time adjusting stitch count to 55 (59, 63, 67) sts. Work (k1tbl, p1) over first 9 (11, 13, 15) sts, ending with k1tbl. Work cable pattern following Chart II over 37 sts and then (k1tbl, p1) to end of rnd.

Shape Sleeve: On every 5th rnd, increase 2 sts centered on underarm until there are 109 (115, 121, 131) sts. Work new sts as p1, k1tbl. Work without further shaping until sleeve is 19 (19¼, 19¾, 20) in / 48 (49, 50, 51) cm long. Divide sleeve at center of underarm and continue back and forth.

Sleeve Cap: BO 6 sts at each side. Then, at each side, on every other row, BO 2 sts 2 times and 1 st 4 times. On every 4th row: BO 1 st 3 (3, 4, 4) times. Work 4 rows and then BO 10 sts at beginning of each of next 6 rows. BO rem sts. Set first sleeve aside while you knit second sleeve the same way.

FINISHING

Weave in all ends neatly on WS. *Gently* steam press sweater on WS under a damp pressing cloth.

Neckband: With smaller circular and two strands of Color 1 (Kidsilk Haze) held together, pick up and

CHART I

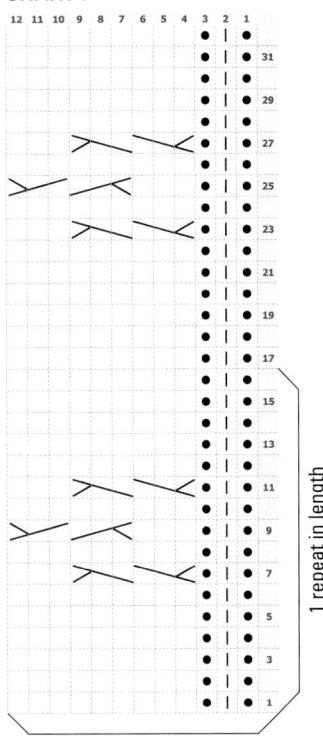

1 repeat = 12 sts

CHART II

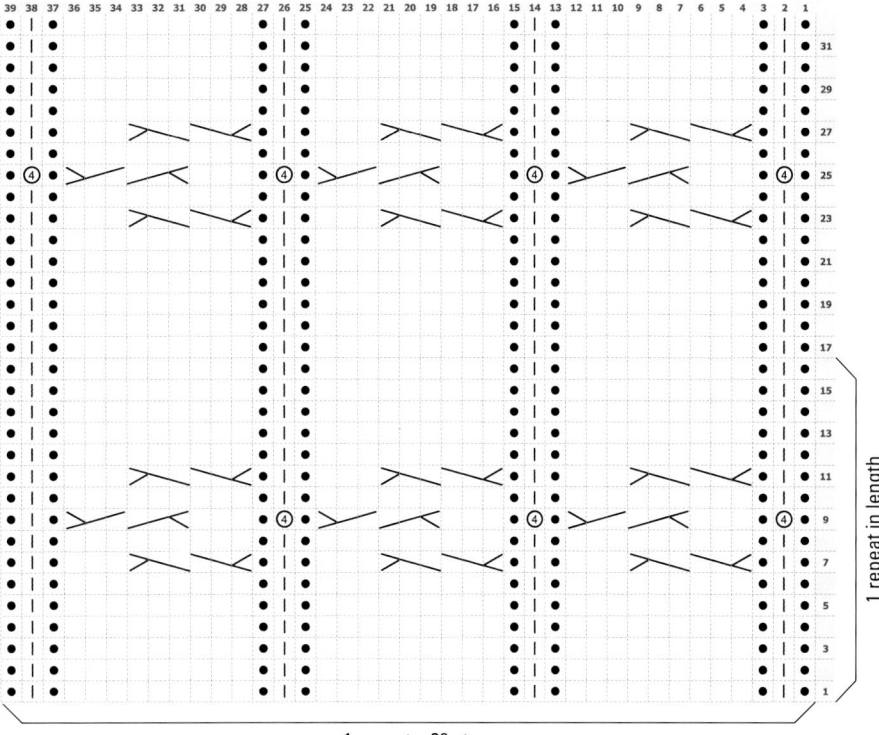

1 repeat = 39 sts

CHART III

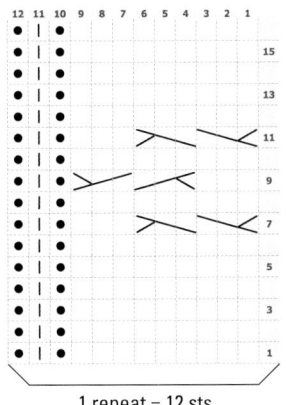

1 repeat = 12 sts

Symbols Key

•	Purl on RS, knit on WS
ǀ	Knit tbl on RS, purl tbl on WS
□	Knit on R, purl on WS
⟩⟨	Place 3 sts on cable needle and hold in front of work, k3, k3 from cable needle.
④	Work (k1, p1, k1, p1) in same st by working alternately into front and back loops of st; Turn, k4; turn, p4; turn, k4; turn. Sl 2 sts to right needle, p2tog and pass the 2 slipped sts over = 1 st again. Pull yarn so knot lies on RS.
⟩⟨	Place 3 sts on cable needle and hold in back of work, k3, k3 from cable needle.

knit 72 (74, 76, 78) sts along front neck and 58 (60, 62, 64) sts long back neck. Work 1 rnd p1tbl and then knit 8 rnds; BO.
Attach sleeves.
Crocheted Decorative Edging for Neck and Sleeves: With two strands of Color 2 (Concorde) held together and crochet hook, work 1 rnd sl st around purl rnd at lower edge of each sleeve and neckband. If you wish, you can also make bobbles on these edges: With doubled Color 2 yarn and hook, attach yarn with 1 sl st. Work 3 dc into same st, but do not complete last step of each dc; when there are 4 loops on hook, bring yarn through all 4 loops at once (the 3 dc are now joined at top of bobble into 1 st). Work 1 sc at top of bobble. Continue and work bobbles all around edge, spacing evenly around. Cut yarn and fasten off.

Tip: The glitter yarn can easily unravel, so knot it before cutting it.

ZEPHYR

This sweater has just the right name: it's light as a gentle breeze. It's knitted with two yarns for differing textures in the stripes. With set-in sleeves, and a wide, round neck, it's a fantastic garment for beginner knitters.

SKILL LEVEL
Easy

SIZES
S (M, L, XL, XXL)

FINISHED MEASUREMENTS
Chest: 36¼ (38½, 41¼, 43¾, 46½) in / 92 (98, 105, 111, 118) cm
Total Length: 20 (21, 21¾, 22½, 23¼) in / 51 (53, 55, 57, 59) cm
Sleeve Length: 12¾ (13, 13½, 13¾, 14¼) in / 32 (33, 34, 35, 36) cm

MATERIALS
Yarn: CYCA #1 (light fingering) Naturally Yarns New Zealand Amuri 4-ply (75% Merino wool, 25% possum, 262 yd/240 m / 50 g)
and
CYCA #0 (lace) Rauma Plum (70% mohair, 30% nylon, 274 yd/251 m / 25 g)
Yarn Colors and Amounts:
Color 1: Amuri Grey-Pink 4032: 100 (100, 100, 150, 150) g
Color 2: Plum Pink 0037: 75 (75, 75, 100, 100) g
Needles: U. S. sizes 2.5 and 4 / 3 and 3.5 mm: circulars and sets of 5 dpn.

GAUGE
22 sts in stockinette on larger needles = 4 in / 10 cm. Adjust needle size to obtain correct gauge if necessary.

Stripe Pattern:
Knit 2 rnds with Color 1 (Amuri), knit 1 rnd and purl 3 rnds with Color 2 (Plum); rep from * to *.

BODY

The sweater is worked in the round from the bottom up.
With smaller circular and Color 1, CO 204 (216, 232, 244, 260) sts. Join, being careful not to twist cast-on row; pm for beginning of rnd. Work around in k2tbl, p2 ribbing for 1¼ in / 3 cm.
Change to larger circular. Work in stripe pattern as described above until body measures a total of 11 (11½, 11¾, 11¾, 11¾) in / 28 (29, 30, 30, 30) cm. Make sure you don't stretch the garment when measuring—lay it flat.

Divide for Front and Back: Pm at each side = 102 (108, 116, 122, 130) sts each for back and front. Work each side separately.

Back: BO 4 sts at each side for armholes. Next, on every other row, at each side, BO 2 sts 2 times and 1 st 4 (4, 5, 5, 6) times, and then on every 4th row: BO 1 st 3 (3, 4, 4, 4) times. Continue without further shaping until armhole depth is 8 (8¼, 8¾, 9½, 10¼) in / 20 (21, 22, 24, 26) cm.
Now shape neck and shoulders.

Neck Shaping: BO the center 38 (40, 42, 44, 46) sts. Work each side separately.

Shape Shoulder: From outermost edge of shoulder, on every other row, BO 4-4-5 (5-5-5, 5-5-6, 6-6-6, 6-7-7) sts.
At the same time, at neck edge, on every other row: BO 2 sts 2 times. No sts rem. Work opposite side to correspond.

Front: BO 4 sts at each side for armholes. Next, on every other row, at each side, BO 2 sts 2 times and 1 st 4 (4, 5, 5, 6) times, and then on every 4th row, BO 1 st 3 (3, 4, 4, 4) times. Continue without further shaping until armhole depth is 4¼ (4¾, 5¼, 6, 6¾) in / 11 (12, 13, 15, 17) cm.
Now shape neck and shoulders.

Neck Shaping: BO the center 26 (28, 30, 32, 34) sts. Work each side separately. At neck edge, on every other row, BO 2 sts 2 times and then 1 st 6 times.

Shape Shoulder: When at same length as back, from outermost edge of shoulder, on every other row, BO 4-4-5 (5-5-5, 5-5-6, 6-6-6, 6-7-7) sts. No sts rem. Work opposite side to correspond.

SLEEVES

The sleeves are worked in the round. With smaller dpn and Color 1, CO 48 (48, 52, 52, 56) sts. Divide sts onto dpn and join. Work around in k2tbl, p2 ribbing for 1¼ in / 3 cm. Change to larger dpn and work in stripe pattern as described above. On first rnd, increase 1 st in every other st = 72 (72, 78, 78, 84) sts.

Shape Sleeve: Every 1½ in / 4 cm, increase 2 sts centered on underarm 3 (6, 5, 7, 7) times = 78 (84, 88, 92, 98) sts.
Continue without further increases until sleeve is 12¾ (13, 13½, 13¾, 14¼) in / 32 (33, 34, 35, 36) cm long.

Sleeve Cap: BO 4 sts at each side at beginning of next 2 rows. Then, at each side, on every other row, BO 2 sts 2 times and 1 st 5 times. On every 4th row: BO 1 st 3 (3, 4, 4, 4) times. Work 2 rows, and then, at beginning of each of next 10 rows, BO 4 sts. BO rem sts. Set first sleeve aside while you knit second sleeve the same way.

FINISHING

Weave in all ends neatly on WS. Join shoulders.

Neckband: With smaller circular and Color 1, pick up and knit 68 (70, 72, 74, 76) sts along front neck and 52 (54, 56, 58, 60) sts along back neck. Work around in (k2tbl, p2) ribbing for 1¼ in / 3 cm. BO in ribbing.
Attach sleeves.
Gently steam press sweater on WS under a damp pressing cloth.

QUEEN OF HEARTS

Hearts are the focus. This sweater features heart panels in several variations on the lower edges of the sleeves, and gracing the round yoke.

SKILL LEVEL
Intermediate

SIZES
S (M, L, XL, XXL)

FINISHED MEASUREMENTS
Chest: 44 (47¼, 50, 52¾, 57) in / 112 (120, 127, 134, 145) cm
Total Length: 21¼ (21¾, 22, 22¾, 23¾) in / 54 (55, 56, 58, 60) cm
This pullover is relatively wide and short, but you can, of course, make it the length you prefer.
Sleeve Length: approx. 18¼ (18¼, 18½, 18½, 19) in / 46 (46, 47, 47, 48) cm

MATERIALS
Yarn:
CYCA #3 (DK, light worsted) Rowan Felted Tweed (50% Merino wool, 25% alpaca, 25% viscose, 191 yd/ 175 m / 50 g)

Yarn Colors and Amounts:
Color 1: Duck Egg 173: 250 (250, 300, 300, 350) g
Color 2: Peony 183: 50 (50, 50, 100, 100) g
Color 3: Carbon 159: 50 (50, 50, 50, 50) g
Color 4: Frozen 185: 50 (50, 50, 50, 50) g
Color 5: Clay 177: 50 (50, 50, 100, 100) g
Needles: U. S. sizes 2.5 and 4 / 3 and 3.5 mm: circulars and sets of 5 dpn. If you work two-color stranded knitting more tightly than one-color knitting, use U. S. 6 / 4 mm for those sections.

GAUGE
22 sts in stockinette/pattern on larger needles = 4 in / 10 cm.
Adjust needle size to obtain correct gauge if necessary.

BODY

The body is worked in the round from the bottom up. With smaller circular and Color 2, CO 248 (264, 280, 296, 320) sts. Join, being careful not to twist cast-on row; pm for beginning of rnd. Work around in k2tbl, p2 ribbing for 12 rnds. Knit 1 rnd. Change to larger circular (size needed to obtain gauge for two-color knitting). Work in pattern following Chart III. See arrow for where to begin and work 31 (33, 35, 37, 40) rep around and 1 rep in length. After completing charted rows, change to gauge-size circular for single-color stockinette and continue with Color 1 until body measures 12¼ in / 31 cm (all sizes). Pm at each side with 124 (132, 140, 148, 160) sts each for front and back.

Shape Armholes: BO 10 (10, 10, 10, 12) sts on each side as follows: BO 5 (5, 5, 5, 6) sts, knit until 5 (5, 5, 5, 6) sts before next side marker, BO 10 (10, 10, 10, 12) sts, knit until 5 (5, 5, 5, 6) sts before side marker and BO 5 (5, 5, 5, 6) sts. Set body aside while you knit sleeves.

SLEEVES

The sleeves are worked in the round. With smaller dpn and Color 1, CO 48 (48, 52, 52, 56) sts. Divide sts onto dpn and join. Work around in k2tbl, p2 ribbing for 12 rnds. Knit 1 rnd, *at the same time* increasing 11 (13, 11, 13, 13) sts evenly spaced around (= increase in every 4th st) = 59 (61, 63, 65, 69) sts. Change to larger dpn (size needed to obtain gauge for two-color knitting). Work pattern following Chart II. See arrow for center of sleeve and count back to determine first st of rnd. Work 1 pattern rep in length. After completing charted rows, change to circular (size needed to obtain gauge for one-color knitting) and continue with Color 1.

Shape Sleeve: After completing pattern, shape sleeve: Increase 2 sts centered on underarm every 10th rnd until there are 75 (81, 89, 97, 105) sts. Continue without further shaping until sleeve is 18¼ (18¼, 18½, 18½, 19) in / 46 (46, 47, 47, 48) cm long.

Shape Armhole: BO 5 (5, 5, 5, 6) sts, knit until 5 (5, 5, 5, 6) sts rem, BO rem sts.

Set first sleeve aside while you knit second sleeve the same way.

JOINING BODY AND SLEEVES

Place all pieces on circular (size needed to obtain gauge for one-color knitting): front, right sleeve, back, left sleeve = 356 (386, 418, 450, 482) sts total. Knit 1 rnd, decreasing 4 (2, 2, 2, 2) sts evenly spaced around = 352 (384, 416, 448, 480) sts. Pm at each intersection of body and sleeve = 4 markers.

Raglan Shaping: Knit until 2 sts before first marker, k2tog tbl, sl m, k2tog. Decrease the same way at each marker.

Decrease as est on every rnd 2 (4, 5, 6, 8) times = 336 (352, 376, 400, 416) sts rem.

Now decrease for raglan as est on every other rnd a total of 3 (2, 3, 3, 4) times = 312 (336, 352, 376, 384) sts rem.

Yoke Pattern: End raglan shaping—further shaping is incorporated into yoke pattern. Change to circular of size needed to obtain gauge for two-color knitting, and work in pattern following Chart I, with 39 (42, 44, 47, 48) rep around and 1 rep in

CHART I

1 repeat = 8 sts

Begin here

length = 117 (126, 132, 141, 144) sts rem. BO rem sts.

FINISHING

Neckband: With smaller circular and Color 2, pick up and knit 104 (112, 116, 124, 128) sts around neck. Work around in k2tbl, p2 ribbing for 12 rnds and then BO in ribbing. Seam underarms.
Weave in all ends neatly on WS. *Gently* steam press sweater on WS under a damp pressing cloth.

CHART II

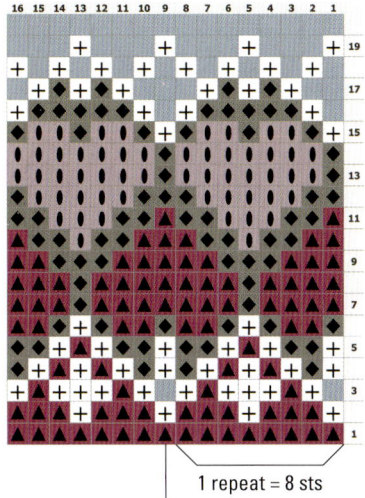

16 15 14 13 12 11 10 9 8 7 6 5 4 3 2 1
19
17
15
13
11
9
7
5
3
1
1 repeat = 8 sts
Center of sleeve

CHART III

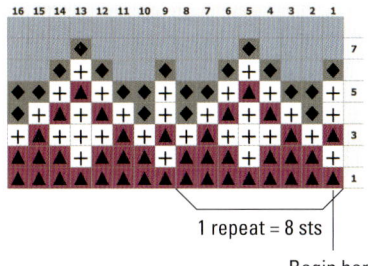

16 15 14 13 12 11 10 9 8 7 6 5 4 3 2 1
7
5
3
1
1 repeat = 8 sts
Begin here

Symbols Key

▒	Color 1
▲	Color 2
◆	Color 3
⬮	Color 4
+	Color 5
⟋	K2tog with Color 2
⟋	K2tog with Color 4
⟋	K2tog with Color 5
▪	No st—st has been decreased away

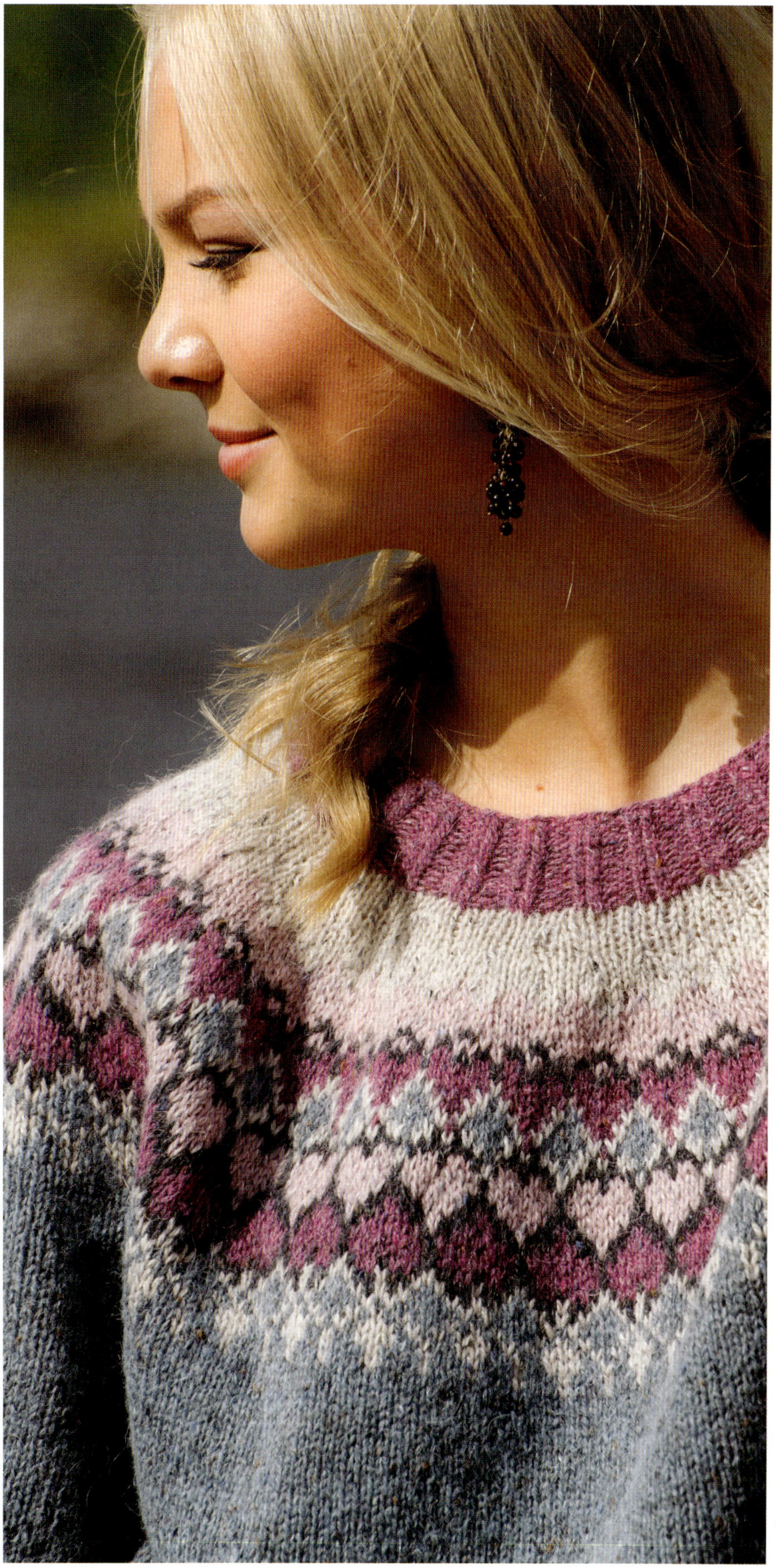

APPLE BLOSSOM

This pullover is a good incentive to practice various techniques: lace, cables, and side increases for batwing shaping. The yarn comes in 150-gram balls, with colors shifting throughout. For that reason, it's important to follow the advice in the pattern for when to knit from each ball as you work.

SKILL LEVEL
Intermediate

SIZES
S (M, L, XL, XXL)

FINISHED MEASUREMENTS
Chest: 36 (37¾, 40¼, 43, 45¼) in / 91 (96, 102, 109, 115) cm
Total Length: approx. 23¾ (24½, 25¼, 26, 26¾) in / 60 (62, 64, 66, 68) cm
Sleeve Length: 14¼ (14½, 15, 15½, 15¾) in / 36 (37, 38, 39, 40) cm

MATERIALS
Yarn:
CYCA #1 (fingering) Mondial Emozione (100% Merino wool, 591 yd/540 m / 150 g)
Yarn Colors and Amounts:
Warm Rose/Sand 758: 450 (450, 600, 600, 600) g
Needles: U. S. sizes 2.5 and 4 / 3 and 3.5 mm: circulars and sets of 5 dpn; cable needle

GAUGE
23 sts in stockinette on larger needles = 4 in / 10 cm. Adjust needle size to obtain correct gauge if necessary.

NOTE: In order for the colors to sequence correctly, it's important that you knit the sleeves first. Begin by working from the outer end of the first ball. When the first sleeve is finished, begin the second sleeve with the outer end of the second ball. Then knit the body. Begin by working from the outer end of the first ball (at the place where you finished first sleeve). When that ball is used up, begin from the inside end on the second ball (the one used for the second sleeve). When that ball is used up, begin with the outer end of a third ball. If you need more yarn, begin with the inside end of a fourth ball.

SLEEVES

The sleeves are worked in the round. See note above for how to begin with the yarn. With smaller dpn, CO 48 (48, 52, 52, 56) sts. Divide sts onto dpn and join. Work around in k3tbl, p1 ribbing for 2½ in / 6 cm. Change to larger dpn and continue in stockinette.
Shape Sleeve: Increase 2 sts centered on underarm every 6th rnd until there are 72 (76, 80, 84, 88) sts. Continue without further shaping until sleeve is 14¼ (14½, 15, 15½, 15¾) in / 36 (37, 38, 39, 40) cm long. BO all sts.
Set first sleeve aside while you knit second sleeve the same way.

BODY

The body is worked in the round from the bottom up. Begin with outer end of first yarn ball (left over after working first sleeve). With smaller circular, CO 224 (256, 268, 284, 304) sts. Join, being careful not to twist cast-on row; pm for beginning of rnd. Work around in k3tbl, p1 ribbing for 3¼ in / 8 cm. Change to larger circular and knit 1 rnd, increasing 2 sts evenly spaced around = 226 (258, 270, 286, 306) sts. Pm at each side = 123 (129, 135, 143, 153) sts each for front and back.
Set Up Pattern: P1, work 7 (8, 9 11, 14) sts in stockinette, 1 cable rep over 32 sts, 43 (47, 51, 55, 59) sts stockinette, 1 cable rep over 32 sts, 7 (8, 9 11, 14) sts stockinette, p1 = front. Set up pattern on back as for front. The two purl sts at each side are side sts; later on, increases are made on each side of these. Work in pattern as est until body measures 8¼ (8¾, 9, 9½, 9¾) in / 21 (22, 23, 24, 25) cm.
Increase on Sides for Sleeves: Now begin increasing 1 st on each of the 2 purl side sts.
At each side: P1, increase 1 in next st, work as est until 1 st rem before purl side sts, increase 1 in this st, p1. Work new sts in stockinette. Increase the same way on every 10th rnd once, on every 8th rnd once, and on every 6th rnd once. Then, increase on every 4th rnd 4 (4, 3, 2, 2) times; on every other rnd 9 (12, 14, 15, 17) times; and then on every rnd 13 (14, 15, 16, 17) times = 181 (195, 205, 215, 231) sts each for front and back. Work 2 rnds.
Now divide work at sides and work front and back separately.
Back: Work back and forth until back measures 5½ (6, 6¼, 6¾, 7) in / 14 (15, 16, 17, 18) cm from split.
Shape Shoulders: Now shape shoulders by binding off from outer edge of shoulders. On every other row, BO 5 sts 14 times (5 sts 8 times and 6 sts 6 times; 5 sts 4 times and 6 sts 10 times; 6 sts 14 times; 6 sts 7 times and 7 sts 7 times).
At the same time, when 3 decrease rows rem, BO the center 33 (35, 37, 39, 41) sts for back neck. Work each side separately. At neck edge, on every other row, BO 2 sts 2 times. No sts rem. Work opposite side to correspond.
Front: Work back and forth until front measures 2 in / 5 cm from split. Now divide front in half and pm on center st = 90 (97, 102, 107, 115) sts for each side of front. Work each side separately.
Right Front: Shape V-neck on every 3rd row: decrease 1 st towards center of front 20 (21, 22, 23, 24) times. *At the same time*, when front is same length as back, shape shoulder as for back.
Left Front: Work as for right front, but reverse shaping to correspond.

FINISHING

Seam shoulders.
Gently steam press sweater on WS under a damp pressing cloth.
Neckband: Use smaller circular and yarn that was used for body. Place center st on needle and pick up and knit 49 (51, 53, 55, 57) sts along right front V-neck, 58 (60, 62, 64, 66) sts along back neck, and 49 (51, 53, 55, 57) sts along left front V-neck. Work 1 rnd k1tbl and then work in k3tbl, p1 ribbing, always working center st at base of V-neck as k1tbl. Work 2 rnds. On next rnd, decrease 1 st at each side of center st. Work 1 rnd without decreasing. Decrease on every other rnd until you've decreased 3 times. BO in ribbing. Attach sleeves.

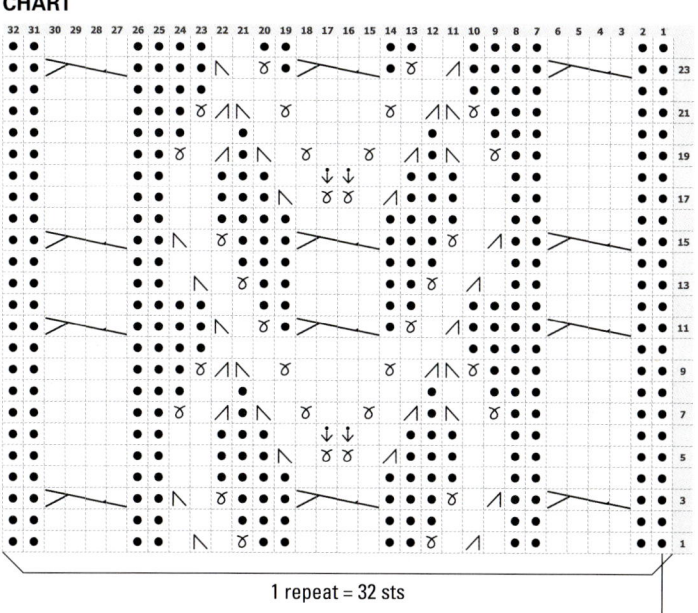

CHART

1 repeat = 32 sts

Begin here

Symbols Key

•	Purl on RS, knit on WS
☐	Knit on RS, purl on WS
╱	K2tog
○	Yo
╲	K2tog tbl
⤫	**Cable over 4 sts:** Place 2 sts on cable needle and hold in front of work, k2, k2 from cable needle.
↓	Work yarnover as k1tbl on both RS and WS

127

FRIDA'S
MIDSUMMER JACKET

A beautiful summer cardigan with many refined details, including lace, rolled edges, and stranded colorwork knitting. This jacket is also easier to knit than it might look. You can wear it over a dress on cool summer days, or to dress up for midsummer festivities.

SKILL LEVEL
Intermediate to Experienced

SIZES
S (M, L, XL, XXL)

FINISHED MEASUREMENTS
Chest: 34¾ (37¾, 41, 43¾, 46½) in / 88 (96, 104, 111, 118) cm
Total Length: 22 (22¾, 23¾, 24½, 25¼) in / 56 (58, 60, 62, 64) cm
Sleeve Length: 19 (19¼, 19¼, 19¾, 19¾) in / 48 (49, 49, 50, 50) cm

MATERIALS
Yarn:
CYCA #1 (fingering) Du Store Alpakka Mini Sterk (40% Merino wool, 40% alpaca, 20% polyamide, 182 yd/166 m / 50 g)
and
CYCA #1 (fingering) Du Store Alpakka Alpakka Wool (60% alpaca, 40% wool, 182 yd/166 m / 50 g)

Yarn Colors and Amounts:
Mini-Sterk:
Color 1: Natural 806: 300 (350, 350, 350, 400) g
Color 2: Yellow-Green 843: 50 (50, 50, 50, 100) g
Color 3: Yellow 835: 50 (50, 50, 50, 50) g
Color 4: Turquoise 834: 50 (50, 50, 50, 50) g
Alpakka Wool:
Color 5: Pink 512: 150 (150, 200, 200, 200) g
Needles: U. S. size 2.5 / 3 mm: 2 32 in / 80 cm circulars and set of 5 dpn.
If you work two-color stranded knitting more tightly than one-color knitting, use U. S. 4 / 3.5 mm for those sections.
Crochet Hook: U. S. size B-1 or C-2 / 2.5 mm
Notions: 6 buttons to match sweater colors; approx. 1.4 yd / 1.3 m ribbon to cover cut steek edges

GAUGE
27 sts in stockinette/pattern = 4 in / 10 cm.
Adjust needle size to obtain correct gauge if necessary.

BODY

The sweater is worked in the round from the bottom up.

Lace Edging at Lower Edge of Jacket: With circular and Color 1, CO 241 (261, 281, 301, 321) sts. Work back and forth in lace pattern, following Chart I, 24 (26, 28, 30, 32) rep + k1. Work 3 rep in length and then set piece aside.

Rolled Edge: With circular and Color 2, CO 241 (261, 281, 301, 321) sts. Work 6 rows back and forth in stockinette.

Joining: Use needle of size necessary to obtain gauge for two-color knitting, and Color 2. Hold rolled edge on top of lace edging and join them with k2tog, joining 1 st from each edge. At end of row, CO 8 sts for center front steek.

Steek: Purl steek sts with Color 1; do not include steek sts in stitch counts.

Join to work in the round.

Pm at each side with 60 (65, 70, 75, 80) sts for each front + 8 steek sts at center front and 121 (131, 141, 151, 161) sts for back. Work around in pattern following Chart II for 1 rep in length. See arrow for beginning st on right front. Next, work pattern following Chart III until body measures a total of 12¾ (13, 13½, 13¾, 13¾) in / 32 (33, 34, 35, 35) cm.

Shape Armholes at Each Side: Knit until 4 (4, 4, 5, 5) sts before side marker, BO 8 (8, 8, 10, 10) sts, knit until 4 (4, 4, 5, 5) sts before side marker, BO 8 (8, 8, 10, 10) sts, knit to end of rnd. On next rnd, CO 6 sts above each armhole gap—steek. Always purl armhole steek sts with Color 1. Continue in pattern following Chart III as est.

Armhole Decreases: On each side of each armhole steek, on every other rnd, decrease 1 st 4 times, and on every 4th rnd, decrease 1 st 3 (3, 4, 4, 5) times.

Beginning about 4 in / 10 cm from total length, work in pattern following Chart IV for rest of body.

At the same time:

Shape V-Neck on Front: On 4th rnd after 1st armhole decrease row, begin shaping V-neck on each side of front steek: K1, work 1 decrease, work around until 3 sts rem, work 1 decrease, k1 on every 3rd rnd 21 (22, 23, 24, 26) times. On right front, decrease with k2tog tbl, and on left front, with k2tog. Continue without further decreases until 1¼ in / 3 cm before total length. BO armhole steek sts at each side and work back and front separately.

Back: BO the center 35 (37, 39, 41, 45) sts for back neck and work each side separately. Decrease at neck edge: on every other row, BO 2 sts 2 times.

At the same time:

Shape Shoulder: On every other row, BO 8-8-8 (9-9-10, 10-10-11, 11-11-11, 11-12-12) sts. No sts rem at shoulder. Work opposite side to correspond.

Front: Shape shoulders as for back. BO rem sts.

SLEEVES

Lace Edging at Lower Edge of Sleeve: With U. S. 2.5 / 3 mm needle and Color 1, CO 61 (61, 71, 71, 71) sts. Work back and forth in lace

CHART I

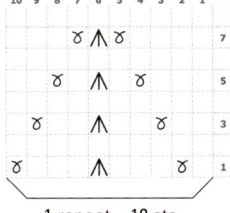

1 repeat = 10 sts

Symbols Key for Chart I

	Knit on RS, purl on WS
○	Yo
⋀	Slip 1, k2tog, psso

CHART II

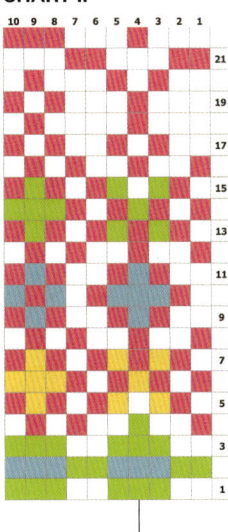

Begin here for right front
Center of sleeve

CHART III

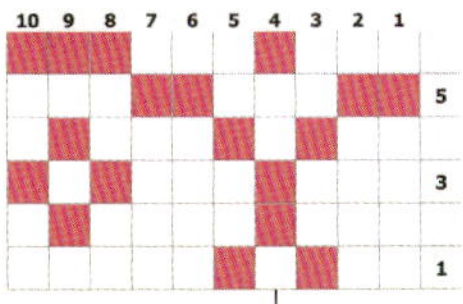

Begin here

Symbols Key or Charts II, III, and IV

	Color 1
▇	Color 2
▇	Color 3
▇	Color 4
▇	Color 5

CHART IV

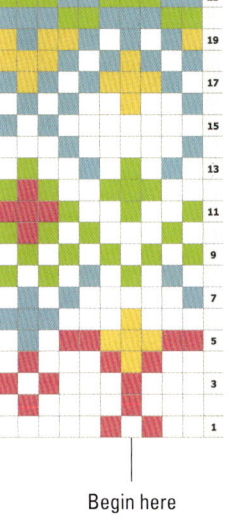

Begin here

pattern, following Chart I, 6 (6, 7, 7, 7) rep + k1. Work 4 rep in length and then set piece aside.
Rolled Edge: With U. S. 2.5 / 3 mm needle and Color 2, CO 61 (61, 71, 71, 71) sts. Work 6 rows back and forth in stockinette.
Joining: Use dpn of size needed to obtain gauge for two-color knitting, and Color 2. Hold rolled edge on top of lace edging and join them with k2tog, joining 1 st from each edge. Divide sts onto dpn and join to work in the round.
Now work pattern following Chart II for 1 rep in length. Count out from arrow at center of sleeve to determine beginning st for your size.

After completing Chart II, work in Chart III pattern for rest of sleeve, making sure the two patterns flow naturally from one to the other. *At the same time*, after joining rolled and lace edges:
Shape Sleeve: On every 6th rnd, increase 2 sts centered on underarm until there are 91 (99, 105, 113, 125) sts. Work new sts into pattern. When sleeve measures a total of 19 (19¼, 19¼, 19¾, 19¾) in / 48 (49, 49, 50, 50) cm, divide sleeve at center of underarm.
Sleeve Cap: Work back and forth. BO 4 (4, 4, 5, 5) sts on each side of sleeve and then, on every other row, BO 2 sts 2 times and then 1 st 5 (6, 7, 7, 8) times. On every 4th row, BO 1 st 4 times. BO 6 sts at beginning of each of next 6 (8, 8, 8, 10) rows. BO rem sts. Make second sleeve the same way.

FINISHING

Weave in all ends neatly on WS. *Gently* steam press sweater on WS under a damp pressing cloth. Machine-stitch 2 lines, zigzag and straight stitch, on each side of center front steek sts and armhole steek sts. Carefully cut open up center of each steek.
Join shoulders.
Crocheted Front Bands: With crochet hook and Color 1, begin at lower right front at join between lace edging and green rolled edge. Work 1 row sc up right front, across back neck, and down left front, ending between rolled edge and lace. Turn and work 1 row sc on WS and then 1 row sc on RS. Work 1 more row sc on WS. When on V-neck on right front, work 1st buttonhole: Ch 3, skip 3 sc, sc in next sc = buttonhole. Space 5 more buttonholes so last buttonhole is 7 sc from beginning of band on lower right front.
After buttonholes are complete, finish row in sc. Turn and work 1 row sc. Work 3 sc in each ch-3 loop. Turn and work 1 row sc and then work 1 row crab st (= sc from left to right). Cut yarn and fasten off.
Sew on 6 buttons to left front band, spaced as for buttonholes.
Sew ribbon on back of front bands to cover cut steek edges.
Seam lace edgings along bottom of jacket and sleeves.

DROP CARDIGAN

A striking jacket with large bobble drops at lower edges of the sleeves and body. This sweater is knitted with super-soft Amuri yarn, which is especially good for texture patterns. You'll want to wear it in summer as well as winter.

SKILL LEVEL
Intermediate

SIZES
S (M, L, XL, XXL)

FINISHED MEASUREMENTS
Chest: 37 (39½, 42¼, 45, 47¾) in / 94 (100, 107, 114, 121) cm
Total Length: 21 (21¾, 22½, 23¼, 24) in / 53 (55, 57, 59, 61) cm
Sleeve Length: 17¼ (17¾, 18¼, 18½, 19) in / 44 (45, 46, 47, 48) cm

MATERIALS
Yarn:
CYCA #1 (light fingering) Naturally Yarns New Zealand Amuri 4-ply (75% Merino wool, 25% possum, 262 yd/240 m / 50 g)
Yarn Colors and Amounts:
Gray-Pink 4032: 300 (300, 350, 350, 400) g
Needles: U. S. sizes 2.5 and 4 / 3 and 3.5 mm circulars and sets of 5 dpn
Notions: 3 buttons to match sweater color

GAUGE
23 sts in ribbing with larger needles = 4 in / 10 cm.
Adjust needle size to obtain correct gauge if necessary.

Bobble Pattern on Body:
5-in-1: Work 5 sts into next st, alternating knitting into front and then back of st.
Row 1 (RS): This row sets up pattern. **Stitch count:** a multiple of 8 + 7 sts.
P3, 5-in-1, p3, k1; rep * until 7 sts rem, p3, 5-in-1, p3.
Rows 2, 4, 6 (WS): *K11, p1*; rep * to * until 11 sts rem, k11.
Rows 3 and 5: *P11, k1*; rep * to * until 11 sts rem, p11.
Row 7: *P3, sl 2 knitwise, p3tog and pass slipped sts over = 1 st, p3, 5-in-1*; rep * to * across until 11 sts rem, p3, sl 2 knitwise, p3tog and pass slipped sts over, p3.
Rows 8, 10, 12 (WS): K3, p1, *k11, p1*; rep * to * until 3 sts rem, k3.
Rows 9 and 11: P3, k1, *p11, k1*; rep * to * across until 3 sts rem, p3.
Row 13 (RS): P3, *5-in-1, p3, sl 2 knitwise, p3tog, pass slipped sts over*; rep * to * until 7 sts rem, p3, 5-in-1, p3.
Rows 14, 16, 18 (WS): *K11, p1*; rep * to * until 11 sts rem, k11.
Rows 15 and 17: *P11, k1*; rep * to * across until 11 sts rem, p11.
Row 19 (RS): *P3, sl 2 knitwise, p3tog, pass slipped sts over (= 1 st), p3, k1*; rep * to * until 11 sts rem, p3, sl 2 knitwise, p3tog, pass slipped sts over (= 1 st), p3.
After completing pattern, work knit over knit and purl over purl for rest of work.
Bobble Pattern on Sleeves:
Work Rows 2-13 of Bobble Pattern above 2 times, and end with Rows 14-19. After completing Bobble Pattern, work knit over knit and purl over purl.

BODY
The body is worked back and forth from the bottom up. With smaller circular, CO 215 (231, 247, 263, 279) sts and knit 4 rows. Change to larger circular and work bobble panel for body as described above. After completing pattern, work knit over knit and purl over purl for rest of body. When body measures 12¼ (12¾, 13, 12¾, 12¾) in / 31 (32, 33, 32, 32) cm, divide body for front and back: Count 53 (57, 61, 65, 69) sts = right front; pm. Count 109 (117, 125, 133, 141) sts = back; pm. Count 53 (57, 61, 65, 69) sts = left front. Work each piece separately.
Back: BO 4 sts at each side for armholes and then, on every other row, BO 2 sts 2 times and 1 st 4 (4, 5, 5, 6) times, and on every 4th row, BO 1 st 3 (3, 4, 4, 4) times. Continue without further shaping until armhole depth is 8 (8¼, 8¾, 9½, 10¼) in / 20 (21, 22, 24, 26) cm. Now shape neck and shoulders:
Shape Neck: BO the center 37 (39, 41, 43, 45) sts for back neck. Work each side separately.
Shape Shoulder: From outer edge of shoulder, on every other row, BO 5-6-6 (6-7-7, 7-7-7, 8-8-8, 8-9-9) sts. *At the same time*, at neck edge, on every other row, BO 2 sts 2 times. No sts rem. Work other side to correspond.
Right Front: BO 4 sts at left side for armhole and then, on every other row, 2 sts 2 times and 1 st 4 (4, 5, 5, 6) times, and on every 4th row, BO 1 st 3 (3, 4, 4, 4) times. Continue without further shaping until armhole depth is 5¼ (5½, 6, 6¾, 7½) in / 13 (14, 15, 17, 19) cm. Now shape neck and shoulders:
Shape Neck: BO 11 (12, 13, 14, 15) sts on right side of front for neck, and then, at neck edge, on every other row, BO 2 sts 2 times and 1 st 6 times.
Shape Shoulder: When at same length as back, from outer edge of shoulder, on every other row, BO 5-6-6 (6-7-7, 7-7-7, 8-8-8, 8-9-9) sts. No sts rem.
Left Front: Work as for right front, reversing shaping to correspond.

SLEEVES
The sleeves are worked back and forth from the bottom up. With smaller needle, CO 55 (55, 63, 63, 71) sts and knit 4 rows. Change to larger needle and work bobble panel for sleeve as described above. After completing pattern, work knit over knit and purl over purl for rest of sleeve.
Shape Sleeve: After completing bobble panel, increase 1 st at each side on every 7th row until there are 83 (87, 93, 99, 105) sts. Work new sts into ribbing pattern. Continue without further shaping until sleeve is 17¼ (17¾, 18¼, 18½, 19) in / 44 (45, 46, 47, 48) cm long.
Shape Sleeve Cap: BO 4 sts at beginning of next 2 rows. Next, on every other row at each side, BO 2 sts once and 1 st 5 times. On every 4th row, BO 1 st 3 (3, 4, 4, 5) times. Work 4 (4, 2, 2, 2) rows and then BO 6 sts at beginning of next 8 (8, 10, 10, 10) rows. BO rem sts. Make second sleeve the same way.

FINISHING
Weave in all ends neatly on WS. *Gently* steam press sweater on WS under a damp pressing cloth.
Seam shoulders.
Left Front Band: With smaller circular and RS facing, pick up and knit 108 (113, 118, 123, 128) sts along left front. Work 1 row k1tbl and then, in garter st, knit 10 rows

back and forth; BO. Mark spacing of 3 buttons on left band, with the top one 2 sts from top of edge and the next 2 spaced 2 in / 5 cm apart.

Right Front Band: Work as for left band, but on Row 5, make buttonholes spaced to match buttons. For each buttonhole: k2tog, yo twice, k2tog tbl. On next row, work each yarnover as k1tbl. Work a total of 10 knit rows and then BO.

Neckband: With smaller circular and RS facing, beginning at right front band, pick up and knit 36 (38, 40, 42, 44) sts along right band and front, 47 (50, 53, 56, 59) sts along back neck, and 36 (38, 40, 42, 44) sts along left front and band. Knit 10 rows and BO.

Attach sleeves and sew on buttons.

DELFT

The world just gets smaller and smaller. A few years ago, I put this design on Facebook and mentioned that it was inspired by Dutch porcelain—and wow, I got masses of requests from Holland to have the pattern translated into Dutch. Delft is a lovely everyday pullover with elegant motifs and a texture pattern forming a lovely combination, with rolled edges, set-in sleeves, and a round neck.

SKILL LEVEL
Intermediate to Experienced

SIZES
S (M, L, XL, XXL)

FINISHED MEASUREMENTS
Chest: 35½ (37¾, 40¼, 45¾, 50½) in / 90 (96, 102, 116, 128) cm
Total Length: 23¾ (24, 24½, 25¼, 26) in / 60 (61, 62, 64, 66) cm
Sleeve Length: 18½ (19, 19¼, 19¾, 19¾) in / 47 (48, 49, 50, 50) cm

MATERIALS
Yarn:
CYCA #3 (DK, light worsted) Rowan Felted Tweed (50% Merino wool, 25% alpaca, 25% viscose, 191 yd/175 m / 50 g)
Yarn Colors and Amounts:
Color 1: Putty 177: 150 (200, 200, 200, 250) g
Color 2: Blue Heather 178: 150 (150, 200, 200, 250) g
Color 3: Thunder Blue 173: 100 (100, 150, 150, 150) g
Needles: U. S. sizes 2.5 and 4 / 3 and 3.5 mm: circulars and sets of 5 dpn.
If you work two-color stranded knitting more tightly than one-color knitting, use U. S. 6 / 4 mm for those sections.

GAUGE
22 sts in stockinette/pattern with larger needle = 4 in / 10 cm.
Adjust needle size to obtain correct gauge if necessary.

BODY

The body is knitted in the round from the bottom up. With smaller circular and Color 3, CO 202 (214, 230, 258, 282) sts. Knit 1 row on WS. Turn and join, being careful not to twist; pm for beginning of rnd. Knit 6 rnds. Pm at each side with 101 (107, 115, 129, 141) sts each for front and back. Change to larger circular (size needed to obtain gauge for two-color knitting). Work in pattern following Chart I, beginning at arrow for your size. Work in pattern to side marker. Begin again at arrow and knit to end of rnd. Work 1 rep in length and then follow Chart II, beginning at arrow for your size.

NOTE: Begin on Row 2 of Chart II and work through Row 17; then rep Rows 1-17.

When body is approx. 14½ in / 37 cm long (all sizes) and you are on Chart II, Row 17, divide body at sides at markers. Work front and back separately.

Back: Work in pattern following Chart III. Work 2 rows and then shape armholes.

Shape Armholes: BO 4 (4, 4, 4, 4) sts on each side. On every other row, decrease 1 st 3 times and then on every 4th row, decrease 1 st 1 (1, 3, 2, 3) times = 85 (91, 97, 111, 121) sts rem.

NOTE: On Row 19 of pattern, change to smaller circular. Rep Rows 20-28 for rest of piece.

When back measures 8¼ (8¾, 9, 9½, 10¼) in / 21 (22, 23, 24, 26) cm above first decrease for armholes, and shape neck and shoulders *at the same time:*

Shape Neck: BO the center 33 (35, 37, 39, 41) sts for back neck. Work each side separately. At neck edge, on every other row, BO 2 sts once and then 1 st 2 times.

Shape Shoulder: From outer edge of shoulder, on every other row, BO 7-7-8 (8-8-8, 8-9-9, 10-11-11, 12-12-12) sts. No sts rem on shoulder.

CHART I

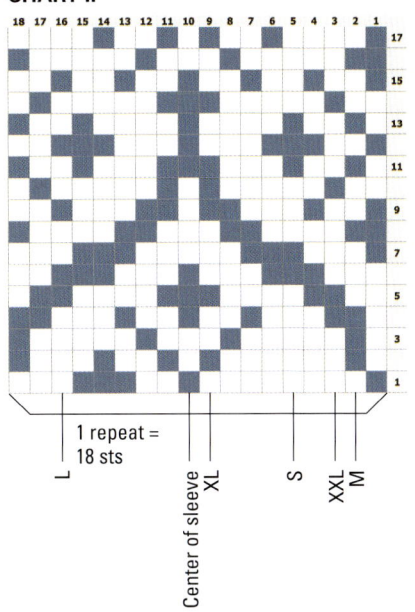

Symbols Key

- ☐ Color 1
- ■ Color 2
- ✚ Knit on RS and purl on WS with Color 3
- • Purl on RS and knit on WS with Color 3

CHART II

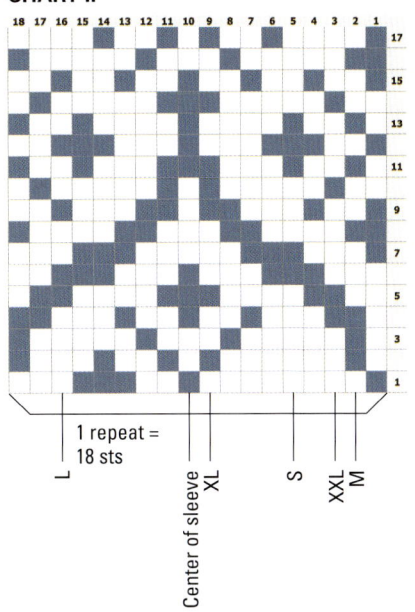

Regarding Chart II:
Begin on Row 2 of chart; work through Row 17, and then repeat Rows 1-17.

CHART III

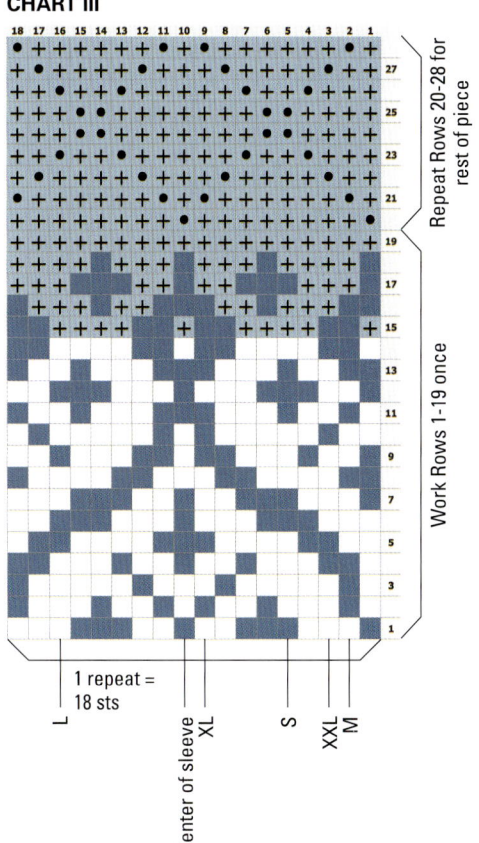

Work other side to correspond.

Front: Work pattern and shape armholes as for back. When armhole depth is 6 (6¼, 6¾, 7, 8) in / 15 (16, 17, 18, 20) cm above first armhole decrease row, BO the center 21 (23, 25, 27, 29) sts for front neck. Work each side separately. At neck edge, on every other row, BO 2 sts 2 times and 1 st 6 times. When at same length as back, shape shoulders as for back.

Set body aside while you knit sleeves.

SLEEVES

The sleeves are worked in the round. With smaller dpn and Color 3, CO 43 (45, 47, 49, 51) sts. Knit 1 row on WS. Turn, divide sts onto dpn and join. Knit 10 (12, 12, 14, 14) rnds. Change to larger dpn (size needed to obtain gauge for two-color knitting). Work pattern following Chart I and begin shaping sleeve on Row 6 of chart (see Shape Sleeve below). See arrow for center of sleeve and count back to determine first st of rnd. Work 1 pattern rep in length following Chart I and then work following Rows 2-17 of Chart II; then rep Rows 1-17. *At the same time:*

Shape Sleeve: Increase 2 sts centered on underarm every 6th rnd until there are 81 (85, 89, 99, 105) sts. Work new sts into pattern. Continue without further shaping until sleeve measures approx. 18½ (19, 19¼, 19¾, 19¾) in / 47 (48, 49, 50, 50) cm. Make sure you end on Row 17 of Chart II. Now work pattern following Chart III and then knit 2 rnds. Divide sleeve at center of underarm and work back and forth, *at the same time* continuing Chart II pattern. On Row 19 of chart, change to smaller needles. Rep Rows 20-28 of chart for rest of sleeve.

Shape Sleeve Cap: BO 4 sts at beginning of next 2 rows. Then, on every other row, BO 2 sts once and 1 st 5 times. On every 4th row, BO 1 st 3 (3, 4, 4, 4) times. After last decrease row, work 6 rows and then BO 4 sts at beginning of next 8 rows. BO rem sts.

Set first sleeve aside while you knit second sleeve the same way.

FINISHING

Join shoulders.

Weave in all ends neatly on WS. *Gently* steam press sweater on WS under a damp pressing cloth.

Neckband: With smaller circular, RS facing, and Color 3, pick up and knit 70 (72, 74, 76, 78) sts along front neck and 48 (50, 52, 54, 56) sts along back neck. Work 1 rnd p1t-bl and then 8 rnds stockinette; BO. Attach sleeves.

HAGIA SOPHIA

A gorgeous pullover with delicate patterning on the body and yoke. This sweater has set-in sleeves and a pattern inspired by Dutch porcelain. I designed three garments to create a series—see the Delft pullover on page 139 and the Oasis jacket on page 27.

SKILL LEVEL
Intermediate to Experienced

SIZES
S (M, L, XL, XXL)

FINISHED MEASUREMENTS
Chest: 35½ (37½, 39¾, 44, 48¾) in / 90 (95, 101, 112, 124) cm
Total Length: 24 (24½, 24¾, 25¼, 26) in / 61 (62, 63, 64, 65) cm
Sleeve Length: 18½ (18½, 18½, 18½, 18½) in / 47 (47, 47, 47, 47) cm

MATERIALS
Yarn:
CYCA #3 (DK, light worsted) Rowan Felted Tweed (50% Merino wool, 25% alpaca, 25% viscose, 191 yd/175 m / 50 g)

Yarn Colors and Amounts:
Color 1: Stone 190: 150 (150, 200, 200, 250) g
Color 2: Ancient 172: 150 (150, 200, 200, 250) g
Color 3: Clay 177: 100 (100, 100, 150, 150) g
Color 4: Cumin 193: 100 (100, 150, 150, 150) g
Needles: U. S. sizes 2.5 and 4 / 3 and 3.5 mm: circulars and sets of 5 dpn.
If you work two-color stranded knitting more tightly than one-color knitting, use U. S. 6 / 4 mm for those sections.

GAUGE
22 sts in stockinette/pattern with larger needle = 4 in / 10 cm.
Adjust needle size to obtain correct gauge if necessary.

CHART I

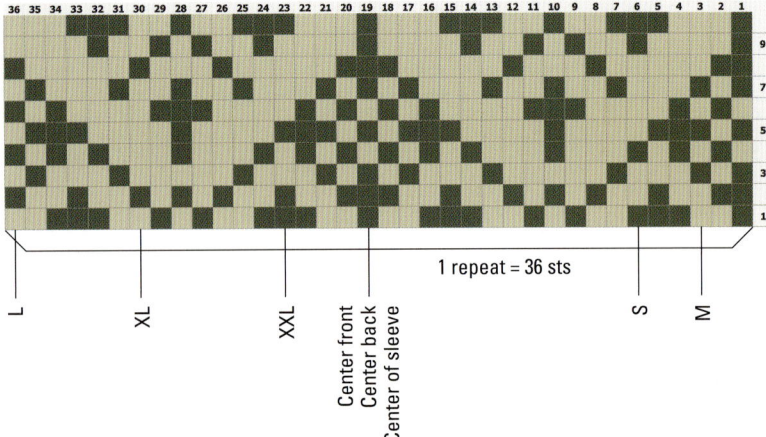

1 repeat = 36 sts

CHART II

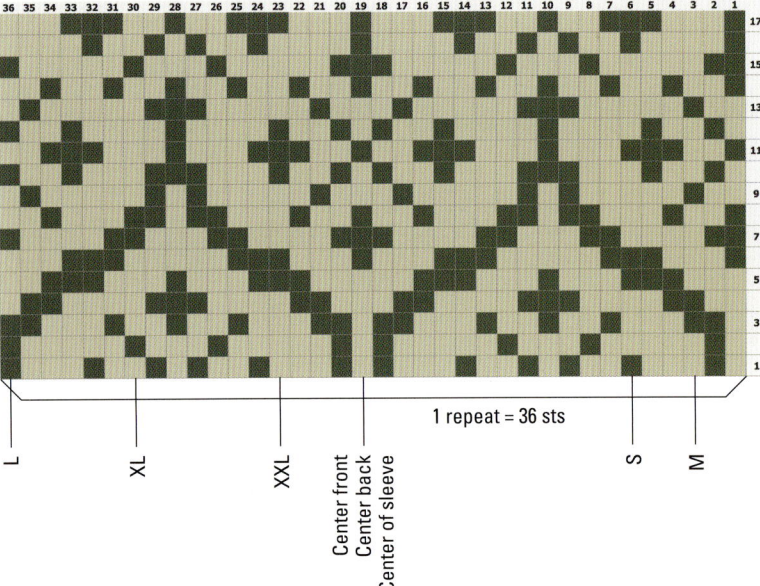

1 repeat = 36 sts

BODY

The body is knitted in the round from the bottom up. With smaller circular and Color 4, CO 198 (210, 222, 246, 274) sts. Join, being careful not to twist cast-on row; pm for beginning of rnd. Knit 7 rnds, purl 3 rnds, knit 1 rnd = rolled edge. Pm at each side with 99 (105, 111, 123, 137) sts each for front and back. Change to larger circular (size needed to obtain gauge for two-color knitting). Work in pattern following Chart I, beginning at arrow for your size. Work in pattern to side marker = front. Work pattern the same way for back. Work 1 rep in length and then follow Chart II, working 5 (5, 5, 6, 6) rep in length. When body measures approx. 15½ (15½, 15½, 18¼ 18¼) in / 39 (39, 39, 46, 46) cm, work in pattern following Chart III, for 1 rep in length. Make sure Chart III pattern flows naturally from Chart II pattern, beginning at arrow for your size as on Chart II. After completing rep, change to circular of size needed to obtain gauge for one-color knitting and work rest of body with Color 3.

At the same time, divide body for front and back after completing all reps of Chart II.

Front:

Shape Armholes: BO 4 (4, 4, 4, 4) sts on each side. On every other row, decrease 1 st 3 times, and then on every 4th row, decrease 1 st 1 (1, 2, 2, 3) times.

Shape Neck: When armhole depth is 5 (6¼, 6¾, 7½, 8¼) in / 15 (16, 17, 19, 21) cm, BO the center 17 (19, 21, 23, 25) sts for front neck. Work each side separately. At neck edge, on every other row, BO 2 sts 2 times and then 1 st 6 (6, 6, 7, 7) times.

At the same time, when 1¼ in / 3 cm before total length:

Shape Shoulders: From outer edge of shoulder, on every other row, BO 8-8-9 (9-9-9, 9-9-10, 10-11-11, 12-12-13) sts. No sts rem on shoulder. Work other side to correspond.

Back: Work as for front until piece is 8 (8¼, 8¾, 9½, 10¼) in / 20 (21, 22, 24, 26) cm above division of body. BO the center 25 (27, 29, 33, 35) sts and work each side separately. At neck edge, on every other row, BO 2 sts 1 time, and then 1 st 2 times.

Shape Shoulders: When back is at same length as front, shape shoulders as for front. No sts rem. Work other side to correspond.

Set body aside while you knit sleeves.

SLEEVES

The sleeves are worked in the round. With smaller dpn and Color 4, CO 45 (49, 49, 51, 51) sts. Divide sts onto dpn and join. Knit 10 rnds, purl 4 rnds, knit 1 rnd = rolled lower edge.

Pattern: Change to larger dpn (size needed to obtain gauge for two-color

CHART III

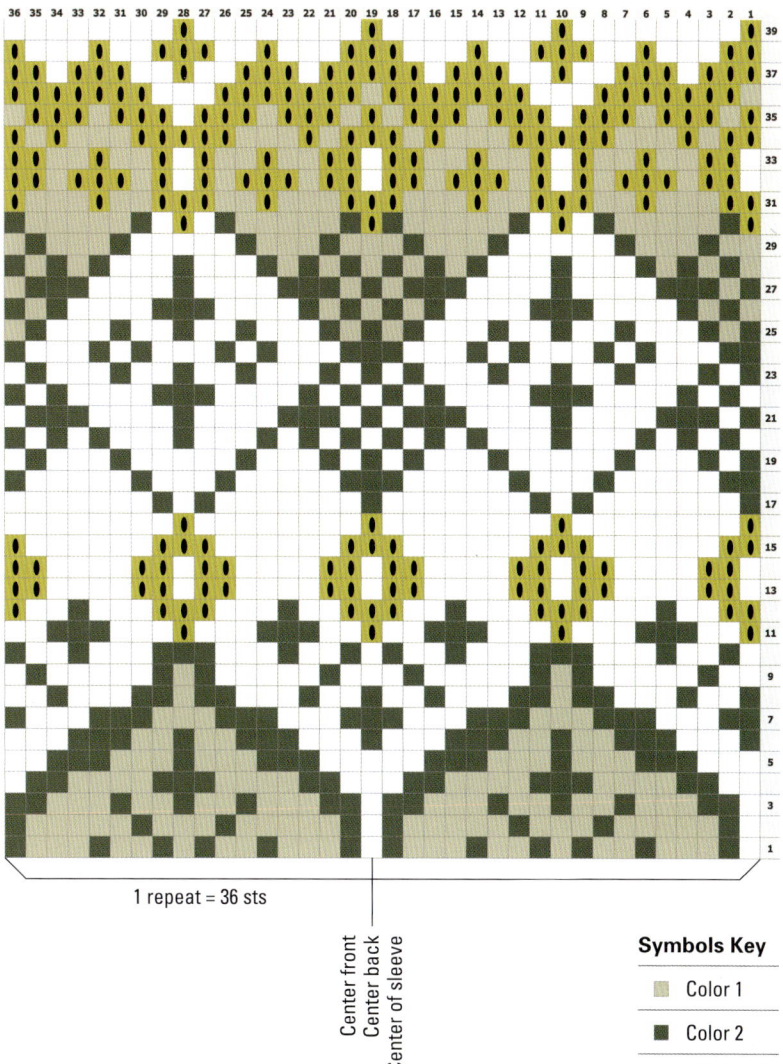

1 repeat = 36 sts

Center front
Center back
Center of sleeve

Symbols Key
- Color 1
- Color 2
- Color 3
- Color 4

knitting). Work pattern following Chart I. See arrow for center of sleeve and count back to determine first st of rnd. *At the same time* as you begin pattern, begin sleeve shaping (see below). Work 1 pattern rep in length following Chart I and then work following Chart II. See arrow for center of sleeve and place pattern so it follows naturally from Chart I pattern. Work Chart II pattern for 6 rep in length.

At the same time:

Shape Sleeve: When you begin working pattern, increase 2 sts centered on underarm every 6th rnd until there are 85 (89, 93, 101, 109) sts. Work new sts into pattern. After completing 6 rep in length, divide sleeve at center of underarm and work back and forth. Work in pattern following Chart III. See arrow for center of sleeve and count back to determine first st of rnd.

Shape Sleeve Cap: BO 4 sts at beginning of next 2 rows. Then, on every other row, BO 2 sts once and 1 st 5 (5, 5, 6, 6) times. On every 4th row, BO 1 st 5 times. BO 4 sts at beginning of next 8 rows. BO rem sts. Set first sleeve aside while you knit second sleeve the same way.

FINISHING

Join shoulders.
Weave in all ends neatly on WS.
Gently steam press sweater on WS under a damp pressing cloth.
Join shoulders.

Neckband: With smaller circular, RS facing, and Color 4, pick up and knit approx. 113 (117, 121, 125, 129) sts around neck. Join, work 1 rnd p1tbl and then 7 rnds stockinette; BO. Let edge roll forward. Attach sleeves.

OLIVIA

A design that focuses on fit. The ribbing on the sides of this soft pullover narrows diagonally into a cabled section under the armholes. This creates a gentle A-line, so the sweater fits just about everybody perfectly.

SKILL LEVEL
Intermediate

SIZES
S (M, L, XL, XXL)

FINISHED MEASUREMENTS
Chest: 34¾ (37, 39½, 43¼, 47¼) in / 88 (94, 100, 110, 120) cm
Total Length: 26 (26¾, 27½, 28¼, 29¼) in / 66 (68, 70, 72, 74) cm
Sleeve Length: 15¾ (16¼, 16¼, 16½, 16½) in / 40 (41, 41, 42, 42) cm

MATERIALS
Yarn:
CYCA #1 (fingering) Du Store Alpakka Tynn Alpakka (100% alpaca, 183 yd/167 m / 50 g)

If Tynn Alpakka is not available, you can substitute Mini Sterk or Alpakka Wool instead.
and
CYCA #1 (light fingering) Du Store Alpakka Dreamline Air (78% Suri alpaca, 22% polyamide, 257 yd/235 m / 25 g)
Yarn Colors and Amounts:
Tynn Alpakka: Soft Old Rose 124: 300 (350, 350, 400, 450) g
Air: Beige DL119: 125 (125, 150, 150, 175) g
The sweater is worked with one strand of each yarn held together.
Needles: U. S. size 4 / 3.5 mm: circulars and sets of 5 dpn; cable needle

GAUGE
21 sts in stockinette with 2 strands of yarn held together = 4 in / 10 cm.
Adjust needle size to obtain correct gauge if necessary.

Seed Stitch:
Rnd 1: *K1, p1*; rep * to * around.
Rnd 2: Work purl over knit and knit over purl.
Rep Rnd 2 for all subsequent rnds.

BODY

Holding one strand of each yarn together, with circular, CO 228 (240, 252, 272, 292) sts. Join, being careful not to twist cast-on row; pm for beginning of rnd. Knit 1 rnd, purl 1 rnd.

Now work in ribbing and seed st as follows:

½ side panel on front, 20 sts: P2, (k2, p4) 3 times; pm.
Center panel on front: Work in seed st over next 74 (80, 86, 96, 106) sts; pm.
Side panel on front and back, 40 sts: Work (p4, k2) 6 times and end with p4; pm.
Center panel on back: Work in seed st over next 74 (80, 86, 96, 106) sts; pm.
½ side panel on back, 20 sts: (P4, k2) 3 times, p2; pm.

Work as est for 6 rnds.
Next Rnd: Continue side panels as est, but purl the 74 (80, 86, 96, 106) sts of center front and back panels. Now work center panels in stockinette. Continue as est until body measures 8¾ (9, 9½, 9½, 9½ in / 22 (23, 24, 24, 24) cm.
Shape Side Panels: Decrease 1 st in each purl column = 14 sts decreased around.
Work without decreasing until body measures 12¾ (13, 13½, 13½, 13½) in / 32 (33, 34, 34, 34) cm. Decrease 1 st in each purl column = 14 sts decreased around and 200 (212, 224, 244, 264) sts rem. Work 1 rnd as est.
Cables: Work cables following chart, beginning at arrow for first ½ side panel and working to end of chart = 13 sts.
Work in stockinette to next side panel and work across chart = 26 sts. Work in stockinette to last ½ side panel and begin at arrow for second side panel with cable over 13 sts. Work 1 chart rep in length.

Divide for Front and Back: Divide body between 13th and 14th sts on chart = 100 (106, 112, 122, 132) sts each for front and back. Work each side separately.

Back: Continue back and forth with stockinette in center panels and ribbing as on last row of chart.
Shape Armholes: BO 5 sts at each side. Then, on every other row, decrease 1 st 4 times, and on every 4th row, decrease 1 st 4 times. Continue in stockinette without further shaping until armhole depth measures 8½ (8¾, 9, 9¾, 10¾) in / 21 (22, 23, 25, 27) cm. Now shape neck and shoulders *at the same time*:
Shape Neck: BO the center 32 (34, 36, 38, 40) sts for back neck. Work each side separately. At neck edge, on every other row, BO 2 sts 2 times.
Shape Shoulders: From outer edge of shoulder, on every other row, BO 5-6-6 (6-6-7, 7-7-7, 8-8-9, 9-10-10) sts. No sts rem on shoulder. Work other side to correspond.
Front: Work as for back until armhole depth is 5½ (6, 6¼, 7, 8) in / 14 (15, 16, 18, 20) cm.
Shape Neck: BO the center 20 (22, 24, 26, 28) sts for front neck. Work each side separately. At neck edge, on every other row, BO 2 sts 2 times and 1 st 6 times.
When at 1¼ in / 3 cm before total length, shape shoulder as for back. No sts rem on shoulder. Work other side to correspond.

SLEEVES

Holding one strand of each yarn together, with dpn, CO 48 (50, 52, 56, 60) sts. Divide sts onto dpn; pm for beginning of rnd. Knit 1 rnd, purl 1 rnd. Set up seed st and cable pattern: Work 17 (18, 19, 21, 23) seed sts, work first 14 sts of chart = center sts, and then 17 (18, 19, 21, 23) seed sts. Work 6 rnds as est. Purl 1 rnd and then work in stockinette over the 17 (18, 19, 21, 23) side sts on each side of center sts instead of seed st.
Shape Sleeve: On every 5th rnd after start of sleeve, increase 2 sts centered on underarm until there are 80 (84, 88, 96, 100) sts. Work new sts in stockinette. Continue until sleeve is 15¾ (16¼, 16¼, 16½, 16½) in / 40 (41, 41, 42, 42) cm long. Divide sleeve at center of underarm and work back and forth. BO 5 sts st each side of sleeve. Then, on every other row, BO 2 sts once and 1 st 4 (4, 5, 6, 6) times. On every 4th row, BO 1 st 3 times and then BO 5 sts at beginning of next 8 rows. BO rem sts. Make second sleeve the same way.

FINISHING

Join shoulders.
Weave in all ends neatly on WS.
Gently steam press sweater on WS under a damp pressing cloth.
Neckband: With circular, RS facing, and doubled yarn, pick up and knit approx. 64 (66 68, 70, 72) sts along front neck and 40 (42, 44, 46, 48) sts along back neck. Work 1 rnd p1tbl and then 6 rnds seed st. Purl 1 rnd and BO.
Attach sleeves.

CHART

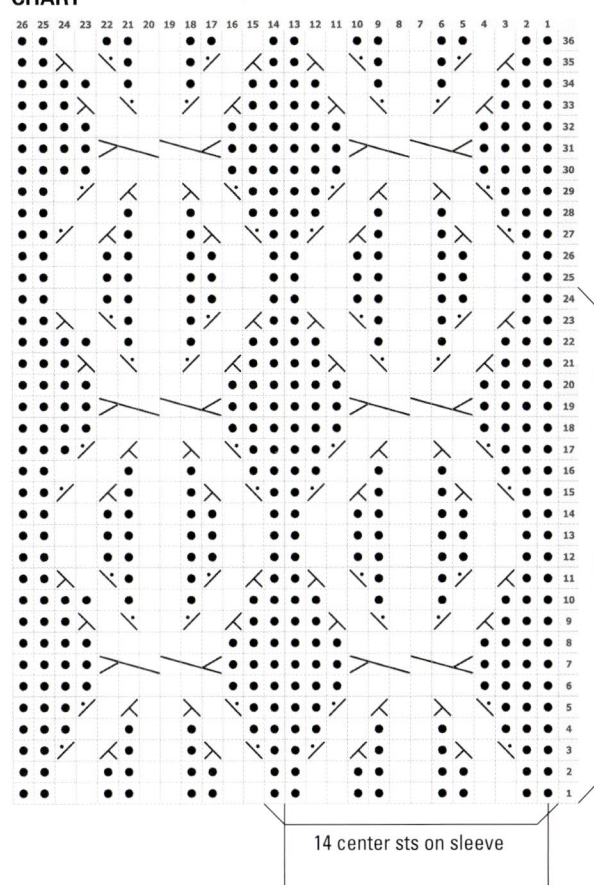

Work Rows 1–24 once on lower edge of sleeve and then repeat row 24 for rest of sleeve

14 center sts on sleeve

Begin working here on 1st side panel, all sizes

Begin working here on 2nd side panel, and on last ½ side panel, all sizes

Symbols Key

☐	Knit on RS, purl on WS
•	Purl on RS, knit on WS
⟍ ⟋	Place 2 sts on cable needle and hold in front of work, p1, k2 from cable needle
⟋ ⟍	Place 1 st on cable needle and hold in back of work, k2, p1 from cable needle
⟍ ⟋	Place 3 sts on cable needle and hold in front of work, k3, k3 from cable needle

CONIFER FOREST

This luscious pullover was inspired by the colors of a conifer forest. It has a round yoke and is oversized. If you want a longer version, you can knit the body longer before you begin the yoke—just remember to buy an extra ball of the main color, if you decide to do this.

SKILL LEVEL
Intermediate

SIZES
S (M, L, XL, XXL)

FINISHED MEASUREMENTS
Chest: 43¾ (47¼, 50, 52¾, 57) in / 111 (120 127, 134, 145) cm
Total Length: approx. 21¼ (21¾, 22, 22¾, 23¾) in / 54 (55, 56, 58, 60) cm
Sleeve Length: 18¼ (18¼, 18½, 18½, 19) in / 46 (46, 47, 47, 48) cm

MATERIALS
Yarn:
CYCA #3 (DK, light worsted) Rowan Felted Tweed (50% Merino wool, 25% alpaca, 25% viscose, 191 yd/175 m / 50 g)

Yarn Colors and Amounts:
Color 1: Lime Green 161: 250 (250, 300, 300, 350) g
Color 2: Grass Green 205: 100 (100, 100, 150, 150) g
Color 3: Ochre Yellow 193: 50 (50, 50, 50, 50) g
Color 4: Burgundy 186 50 (50, 50, 50, 50) g
Needles: U. S. sizes 2.5 and 4 / 3 and 3.5 mm: circulars and sets of 5 dpn
If you work two-color stranded knitting more tightly than one-color knitting, use U. S. 6 / 4 mm for those sections.

GAUGE
22 sts in stockinette/pattern on larger needles = 4 in / 10 cm.
Adjust needle size to obtain correct gauge if necessary.

BODY

The body is worked in the round from the bottom up. With smaller circular and Color 2, CO 244 (264, 280, 296, 320) sts. Join, being careful not to twist cast-on row; pm for beginning of rnd. Work 8 rows in k2, p2 ribbing. Change to Color 4 and knit 1 rnd, purl 1 rnd. Change to Color 3 and knit 1 rnd, purl 1 rnd. Change to Color 1 and knit 1 rnd, purl 1 rnd.

Change to larger circular and continue with Color 1 and stockinette until body measures 12¼ in / 31 cm (all sizes). Pm at each side = 122 (132, 140, 148, 160) sts each for front and back.

Shape Armholes: BO 10 (10, 10, 10, 12) sts at each side as follows: BO 5 (5, 5, 5, 6) sts, knit until 5 (5, 5, 5, 6) sts before next side marker, BO 10 (10, 10, 10, 12) sts, knit until 5 (5, 5, 5, 6) sts rem and BO those sts.

Set body aside while you knit sleeves.

SLEEVES

The sleeves are worked in the round. With smaller dpn and Color 1, CO 48 (48, 52, 52, 56) sts Divide sts onto dpn and join. Work 8 rnds k2, p2 ribbing. Change to Color 4 and knit 1 rnd purl 1 rnd. Change to Color 3 and knit 1 rnd, purl 1 rnd. Change to Color 2 and knit 1 rnd, purl 1 rnd. Change to Color 1 and larger dpn. Continue in stockinette. On first rnd, increase 1 st in every 4th st = 12 (12, 13, 13, 14) sts increased.

Sizes L and XL: Increase 1 more st = 60 (60, 66, 66, 70) sts. Continue in stockinette.

At the same time:

Shape Sleeve: On every 12th (10th, 8th, 8th, 7th) rnd, increase 2 sts centered on underarm until there are 74 (80, 88, 96, 104) sts. When sleeve is 18¼ (18¼, 18½, 18½, 19) in / 46 (46, 47, 47, 48) cm long, shape armholes: BO 5 (5, 5, 5, 6) sts, knit until 5 (5, 5, 5, 6) sts rem, and BO rem sts.

Set first sleeve aside while you knit second sleeve the same way.

JOINING BODY AND SLEEVES

Place all pieces on larger circular: front, right sleeve, back, left sleeve = 352 (384, 416, 448, 480) sts total. Pm at each intersection of body and sleeve = 4 markers.

Raglan Shaping: Knit until 2 sts before first marker, k2tog tbl, sl m, k2tog. Decrease the same way at each marker.

Decrease as est on every rnd 2 (4, 5, 6, 8) times = 336 (352, 376, 400, 416) sts rem.

Now decrease for raglan as est on every other rnd 3 (2, 3, 3, 4) times = 312 (336, 352, 376, 384) sts rem. Knit 1 rnd, decreasing 0 (0, 4, 4, 0) sts evenly spaced around = 312 (336, 348, 372, 384) sts rem.

Yoke Pattern: End raglan shaping—further shaping is incorporated into yoke pattern. Change to circular of size needed to obtain gauge for two-color knitting, and work in pattern following chart, with 26 (28, 29, 31, 32) rep around and 1 rep in length = 104 (112, 116, 124, 128) sts rem. BO rem sts.

FINISHING

Neckband: With smaller circular and Color 2, pick up and knit 1 st in each st around neck = 104 (112, 116, 124, 128) sts. Work 1 rnd k1tbl. Change to Color 4 and knit 1 rnd, purl 1 rnd. Change to Color 3 and knit 1 rnd, purl 1 rnd. Change to Color 2 and knit 1 rnd, purl 1 rnd. Work 9 rnds in k2tbl, p2 ribbing and then BO in ribbing. Seam underarms.

Weave in all ends neatly on WS. *Gently* steam press sweater on WS under a damp pressing cloth.

CHART

1 repeat = 12 sts

Symbols Key

- Color 1
- Color 2
- Color 3
- Color 4
- K2tog with Color 2
- K2tog with Color 3
- No st—st has been decreased away

TALIA

The name "Talia" comes from Hebrew, and it means "dew from heaven." Such a pretty name for a luscious, timeless pullover. This sweater has lace on the lower edges of the body and sleeves, vertical ribbing, raglan shaping, and a round neck with a rolled edge.

SKILL LEVEL
Intermediate

SIZES
S (M, L, XL, XXL)

FINISHED MEASUREMENTS
Chest: 35½ (38½, 41¼, 44, 50) in / 90 (98, 105, 112, 127) cm
Total Length: 24 (24¾, 25½, 26½, 27¼) in / 61 (63, 65, 67, 69) cm
Sleeve Length: 19¼ (19¼, 19¼, 19¾, 19¾) in / 49 (49, 49, 50, 50) cm

MATERIALS
Yarn:
CYCA #1 (light fingering) Naturally Yarns New Zealand Amuri 4-ply (75% Merino wool, 25% possum, 262 yd/240 m / 50 g)
Yarn Colors and Amounts:
Red Heather 4034: 250 (250, 300, 300, 350) g
Needles: U. S. size 2.5 / 3 mm: circulars and sets of 5 dpn; cable needle

GAUGE
25 sts in ribbing = 4 in / 10 cm.
Adjust needle size to obtain correct gauge if necessary.

CHART

1 repeat = 17 sts

Begin body and sleeves here

Symbols Key

☐	Knit on RS, purl on WS
ƍ	Yo
⋀	Sl 1, k2tog, psso
•	Purl on RS, knit on WS
⟩⟨	Place 3 sts on cable needle and hold in back of work, k3, k3 from cable needle
⟨⟩	Place 3 sts on cable needle and hold in front of work, k3, k3 from cable needle
■	No st—st has been decreased away

BODY

The body is worked in the round from the bottom up.
CO 254 (276, 288, 322, 356) sts. Join, being careful not to twist cast-on row; pm for beginning of rnd. Knit 1 rnd, purl 1 rnd, knit 1 rnd, purl 1 rnd. Pm at each side = 127 (138, 144, 161, 178) sts each for front and back.

Set up Pattern: From beginning of rnd, k3 (0, 3, 3, 3), p2, begin at arrow for body and work 17-st rep 7 (8, 8, 9, 10) times, and end with k3 (0, 3, 3, 3) = front. Work back as for front. Rep Rows 1-14 of chart 3 times in length and then work Rows 15-16 of chart.

NOTE: 2 sts are decreased in center of rep on Row 15 of chart = 113 (122, 128, 143, 158) sts rem each for front and back.

Rep Row 16 of chart for rest of body and continue until body measures 15¾ (16¼, 16½, 16½, 17) in / 40 (41, 42, 42, 43) cm.

Shape Armholes: BO 12 sts (all sizes) at each side as follows: BO 6 sts, knit until 6 sts before next side marker, BO 12 sts, knit until 6 sts rem and BO 6 sts.

Set body aside while you knit sleeves.

SLEEVES

The sleeves are worked in the round. With dpn, CO 70 sts (all sizes). Divide st onto dpn and join. Knit 1 rnd, purl 1 rnd, knit 1 rnd, purl 1 rnd. Set up Pattern: From beginning of rnd, p2, begin at arrow for sleeve and work 17-st rep 4 times.
Rep Rows 1-14 of chart 3 times in length and then work Rows 15-16 once. Rep Row 16 of chart for rest of sleeve.

NOTE: 2 sts are decreased in center of rep on Row 15 of chart = 62 sts rem.

Shape Sleeve: After completing 3 rep in length of pattern, begin shaping sleeve: Increase 2 sts centered on underarm every 8th rnd until there are 90 (94, 100, 106, 114) sts. Work new sts into pattern. Continue without further shaping until sleeve is 19¼ (19¼, 19¼, 19¾, 19¾) in / 49 (49, 49, 50, 50) cm long.

Armhole: BO 6 sts, knit until 6 sts rem, BO 6 sts.

Set first sleeve aside and make second sleeve the same way.

JOINING BODY AND SLEEVES

Place all pieces on circular: front, right sleeve, back, left sleeve = 358 (384, 408, 450, 496) sts total. Pm at each intersection of body and sleeve = 4 markers. Work 2 rnds without decreasing.

Raglan Shaping: Knit until 2 sts before first marker, k2tog tbl, sl m, k2tog. Decrease the same way at each marker.

Decrease as est on every rnd 2 (3, 4, 5, 7) times = 342 (360, 376, 410, 440) sts rem.

Now decrease for raglan as est on every 3rd rnd 21 (22, 24, 26, 29) times = 174 (184, 184, 202, 208) sts rem.

Shape Neck: BO the 35 (38, 40, 43, 46) center front sts for neck. Work back and forth. On each side of neck, on every other row, BO 2 sts 2 times and 1 st 2 (2, 3, 3, 3) times. *At the same time*, continue raglan shaping on every (RS) row (= every other row) 7 times until neck shaping is finished.

Neckband: Pick up and knit 72 (74, 76, 78, 80) sts along front neck and 60 (62, 64, 66, 70) sts along back. Work 1 rnd k1tbl, then purl 1 rnd, knit 1 rnd, purl 1 rnd, knit 1 rnd, purl 1 rnd, and knit 5 rnds. BO. Seam underarms.

Weave in all ends neatly on WS. *Gently* steam press sweater on WS under a damp pressing cloth.

LATE AUTUMN

Autumn color leaves surround this gorgeous sweater's yoke, inspired by late fall colors. That's the time of year you'll find me in the forest hunting for mushrooms and berries, and maybe I'll be wearing my Late Autumn pullover.

SKILL LEVEL
Intermediate to Experienced

SIZES
S (M, L, XL, XXL)

FINISHED MEASUREMENTS
Chest: 35½ (38½, 42¼, 48½, 54¾) in / 90 (98, 107, 123, 139) cm
Total Length: 24½ (24¾, 25¼, 26, 26¾) in / 62 (63, 64, 66, 68) cm
Sleeve Length: 19 (19, 19¼, 19¼, 19¼) in / 48 (48, 49, 49, 49) cm

MATERIALS
Yarn:
CYCA #3 (DK, light worsted) Du Store Alpakka Sterk (40% Merino wool, 40% alpaca, 20% polyamide, 150 yd/137 m / 50 g)

Yarn Colors and Amounts:
Color 1: Gray-Black Heather 808: 300 (350, 350, 400, 400) g
Color 2: Black 809: 100 (100, 100, 100, 150) g
Color 3: Green 812: 170: 50 (50, 50, 50, 50) g
Color 4: Golden Yellow 835: 50 (50, 50, 50, 50) g
Color 5: Burnt Copper 862: 50 (50, 50, 50, 50) g
Color 6: Red-Violet 832: 50 (50, 50, 50, 50) g
Needles: U. S. sizes 2.5 and 4 / 3 and 3.5 mm: circulars and sets of 5 dpn.
If you work two-color stranded knitting more tightly than one-color knitting, use U. S. 6 / 4 mm for those sections.

GAUGE
22 sts in stockinette/pattern with U. S. 4 / 3.5 mm or U. S. 6 / 4 mm = 4 x 4 in / 10 x 10 cm.
Adjust needle size to obtain correct gauge if necessary.

BODY

The body is worked in the round from the bottom up.
With smaller circular and Color 1, CO 200 (220, 240, 270, 300) sts. Join, being careful not to twist cast-on row; pm for beginning of rnd. Knit 1 rnd, purl 1 rnd. Change to Color 6 and knit 1 rnd, purl 1 rnd. Change to Color 2 and knit 1 rnd, purl 1 rnd. Change to larger circular for stranded colorwork. Work in pattern following Chart III = 20 (22, 24, 27, 30) rep around and 1 rep in length. Continue with Color 1 in stockinette (with needle of size needed to obtain gauge for one-color knitting). On 1st rnd, increase 8 (6, 4, 0, 6) sts evenly spaced around = 208 (226, 244, 270, 306) sts. Knit until body measures 15¾ in / 40 cm (all sizes). Pm at each side = 104 (113, 122, 135, 153) sts each for front and back.

Shape Armholes: BO 12 (12, 12, 12, 14) sts at each side as follows: BO 6 (6, 6, 6, 7) sts, knit until 6 (6, 6, 6, 7) sts before next side marker, BO 12 (12, 12, 12, 14) sts, knit until 6 (6, 6, 6, 7) sts rem, and BO those last sts. Set body aside while you knit sleeves.

SLEEVES

The sleeves are worked in the round. With smaller dpn and Color 1, CO 51 (51, 55, 59, 63) sts. Divide sts onto dpn and join. Knit 1 rnd, purl 1 rnd. Change to Color 6 and knit 1 rnd, purl 1 rnd. Change to Color 2 and knit 1 rnd, purl 1 rnd. Change to larger dpn for stranded colorwork. Work in pattern following Chart II for 1 rep in length. See arrow for center of sleeve and count back to determine first st of rnd. After completing charted rows, continue in Color 1 and stockinette.

At the same time as working Chart II:
Shape Sleeve: On Row 6 of charted pattern, begin shaping sleeve: Increase 2 sts centered on underarm every 8th rnd until there are 82 (90, 96, 104, 116) sts. Continue without further shaping until sleeve is 19 (19, 19¼, 19¼, 19¼) in / 48 (48, 49, 49, 49) cm long.
Armhole: BO 6 (6, 6, 6, 7) sts, knit until 6 (6, 6, 6, 7) sts rem, BO 6 (6, 6, 6, 7) sts. Set first sleeve aside and make second sleeve the same way.

JOINING BODY AND SLEEVES

Place all pieces on larger circular: front, right sleeve, back, left sleeve = 324 (358, 388, 430, 486) sts total. Continue with Color 1. Pm at each intersection of body and sleeve = 4 markers. Knit 1 rnd, decreasing 0 (8, 4, 2, 8) sts evenly spaced around = 324 (350, 384, 428, 478) sts.
Raglan Shaping: Knit until 2 sts before first marker, k2tog tbl, sl m, k2tog. Decrease the same way at each marker.
Decrease as est on every rnd 0 (1, 3, 4, 6) times = 324 (342, 360, 396, 432) sts rem.
Yoke Pattern: End raglan shaping—further shaping is incorporated into yoke pattern (as shown on chart). Change to circular of size needed to obtain gauge for two-color knitting, and work in pattern following Chart I, with 18 (19, 20, 22, 24) rep around and 1 rep in length = 126 (133, 140, 154, 168) sts rem.
Shape Neck: With Color 2 and smaller circular, knit 1 rnd, decreasing 9 (11, 6, 8, 4) sts evenly spaced around = 117 (122, 134, 146, 164) sts rem. Purl 1 rnd. Change to Color 6 and knit 1 rnd, purl 1 rnd. Change to Color 1 and knit 1 rnd, purl 1 rnd. BO.

FINISHING

Seam underarms.
Weave in all ends neatly on WS.
Gently steam press sweater on WS under a damp pressing cloth.

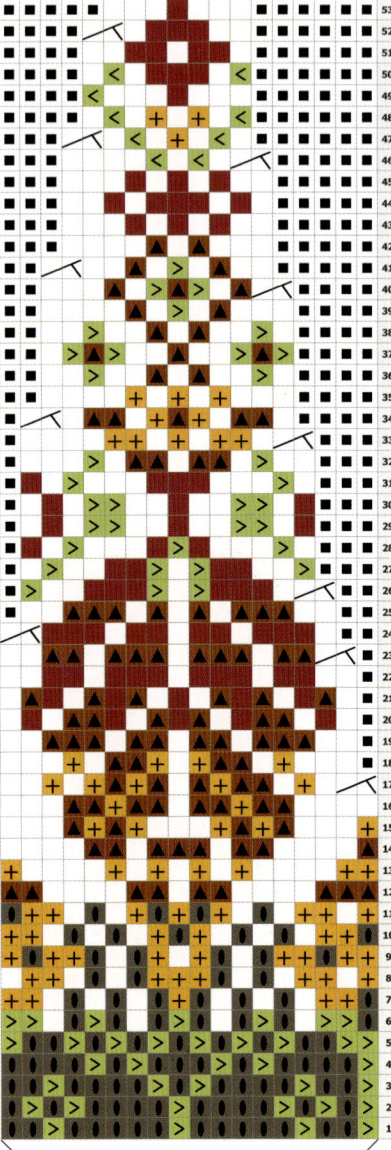

1 repeat = 18 sts

CHART II

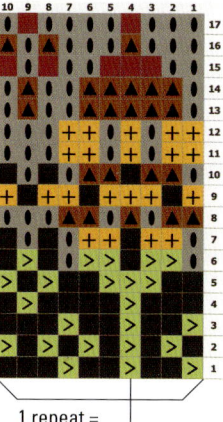

1 repeat = 10 sts
Center of sleeve

CHART III

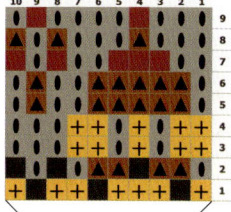

1 repeat = 10 sts

Symbols Key

■	Color 1
□	Color 2 on Chart I
■	Color 2 on Charts II and III
>	Color 3
+	Color 4
▲	Color 5
■	Color 6
⧄	K2tog
▪	No st—st has been decreased away

163

FILIPPA

Not everyone likes ribbing that draws in, so here the ribbing is wider than the sweater itself. On the last round of ribbing, on the lower edges of the body and sleeves, the stitch count decreases, so the ribbing is more like a gentle ruffle. The attractive high neck is also wide and comfortable.

SKILL LEVEL
Intermediate to Experienced

SIZES
S (M, L, XL, XXL)

FINISHED MEASUREMENTS
Chest: 41¾ (45, 48, 52, 56) in / 106 (114, 122, 132, 142) cm
Total Length: 28¼ (29¼, 30, 30¾, 31½) in / 72 (74, 76, 78, 80) cm
Sleeve Length: 19¼ (19¼, 19¾, 19¾, 20) in / 49 (49, 50, 50, 51) cm or desired length

MATERIALS
Yarn:
CYCA #3 (DK, light worsted) Hillesvåg Tinde (100% Norwegian wool, 284 yd/260 m / 100 g)
Yarn Colors and Amounts:
Color 1: Navy Blue 2133: 500 (500, 550, 550, 600) g
Color 2: Dusty Rose 2137: 100 (150, 150, 150, 200) g
Color 3: Lime 2107: 170: 50 (50, 50, 50, 50) g
Color 4: Cognac 2103: 50 (50, 50, 50, 50) g
Needles: U. S. sizes 2.5 and 4 / 3 and 3.5 mm: circulars and sets of 5 dpn.
If you work two-color stranded knitting more tightly than one-color knitting, use U. S. 6 / 4 mm for those sections.

GAUGE
22 sts in stockinette/pattern with U. S. 4 / 3.5 mm or U. S. 6 / 4 mm = 4 x 4 in / 10 x 10 cm.
Adjust needle size to obtain correct gauge if necessary.

BODY

The body is worked in the round from the bottom up.

With smaller circular and Color 1, CO 390 (415, 450, 480, 520) sts. Join, being careful not to twist cast-on row; pm for beginning of rnd. Work around in p3, k2 ribbing for 4 in / 10 cm. On next rnd, reduce stitch count in purl columns: *Sl 1, p2tog, psso, k2*; rep * to * around = 234 (249, 270, 288, 312) sts rem. Purl 3 rnds, and on last rnd, increase 1 st for size M and 2 sts evenly spaced around on sizes XL and XXL = 234 (250, 270, 290, 314) sts. Continue in stockinette.

Stripes: Change to larger circular and work stripes:
Knit 2 rnds with Color 3,
knit 2 rnds with Color 2,
knit 1 rnd with Color 3,
knit 2 rnds with Color 2,
knit 2 rnds with Color 3.
Change to Color 1 and knit 1 rnd, purl 3 rnds.

Pm at each side = 117 (125, 135, 145, 157) sts each for front and back.

Pattern: Change to larger circular (size needed to obtain gauge for two-color knitting) and work pattern following chart, beginning at arrow for your size. Work to marker = front. Work same way on back. Work in pattern until body measures a total of 19 (19¼, 19¾, 19¾, 19¾) in / 48 (49, 50, 50, 50) cm. Now divide for front and back at side markers and work each separately.

Back: Work back and forth with Color 1 on larger circular (size needed to obtain gauge for one-color knitting), beginning on RS.

Shape Armholes: BO 2 sts at beginning of next 8 rows. *At the same time*, knit 2 rows, purl 1 row, knit 1 row (looks like 3 purl rows on RS). Work rest of body in stockinette. Work without further shaping until armhole depth is 8¾ (9, 9½, 10¼, 11) in / 22 (23, 24, 26, 28) cm. Now shape neck and shoulders *at the same time*.

Back Neck: BO the center 31 (33, 35, 37, 39) sts for back neck. Work each side separately. At neck edge, on every other row, BO 2 sts 3 times.

Shape Shoulder: From outer edge of shoulder, on every other row, BO 7-7-7-8 (8-8-8-8, 9-9-9-9, 10-10-10-10, 11-11-11-12) sts. No sts rem on shoulders. Work opposite side to correspond.

Front: Work as for back, but shape neck when 4 in / 10 cm before total length.

Front Neck: BO the center 27 (29, 31, 33, 35) sts for front neck. Work each side separately. At neck edge, on every other row, BO 2 sts 1 time and 1 st 6 times.

Shape shoulder as for back. Work opposite side to correspond.

Set body aside while you knit sleeves.

SLEEVES

The sleeves are worked in the round. With smaller dpn and Color 1, CO 90 (95, 105, 110) sts. Divide sts onto dpn and join. Work around in p3, k2 ribbing for 4 in / 10 cm. On next rnd, reduce stitch count in the purl columns: *Sl 1, p2tog, psso, k2*; rep * to * around = 54 (57, 60, 63, 66) sts rem. Change to larger dpn. Purl 3 rnds, and on last rnd, increase 1 st for sizes S, L, and XXL = 55 (57, 61, 63, 67) sts. Now work stripes in stockinette, and *at the same time* begin shaping sleeve (see "Shape Sleeve" section below).

Stripes:
Knit 2 rnds with Color 3,
knit 2 rnds with Color 2,
knit 1 rnd with Color 3,
knit 2 rnds with Color 2,
knit 2 rnds with Color 3.
Change to Color 1 and knit 1 rnd, purl 3 rnds.

Pattern: Change to larger dpn (size needed to obtain gauge for two-color knitting) and work pattern following chart. See arrow for center of sleeve and count back to determine first st of rnd. Work Rows 10-26 of chart, and then Rows 1-9. Change to Color 1 on larger dpn (size needed to obtain gauge for one-color knitting). Knit 1 rnd, purl 3 rnds and work rest of sleeve in stockinette with Color 1.

Shape Sleeve: Increase 2 sts centered on underarm every 5th rnd until there are 95 (99, 103, 111, 119) sts. Continue without further shaping until sleeve is 19¼ (19¼, 19¾, 19¾, 20) in / 49 (49, 50, 50, 51) cm long. Divide sleeve at center of underarm and work back and forth. BO 2 sts at beginning of next 8 rows and then BO rem sts.

Set first sleeve aside and make second sleeve the same way.

FINISHING

Seam shoulders.

Weave in all ends neatly on WS.

Neckband: With smaller circular and Color 1, pick up and knit 55 (57, 59, 61, 63) sts along front neck and 53 (54, 55, 56, 57) sts along back neck. Work 1 rnd k1tbl and then 6 rnds k2, 1 ribbing. Now increase 1 st in each purl column = k2, p2 ribbing. Continue in k2, p2 ribbing until neck measures 3¼ in / 8 cm total. Again, increase 1 st in each purl column and work in k2, p3 ribbing until neck measures 8¾ in / 22 cm. BO in ribbing.

Attach sleeves.

Gently steam press sweater on WS under a damp pressing cloth.

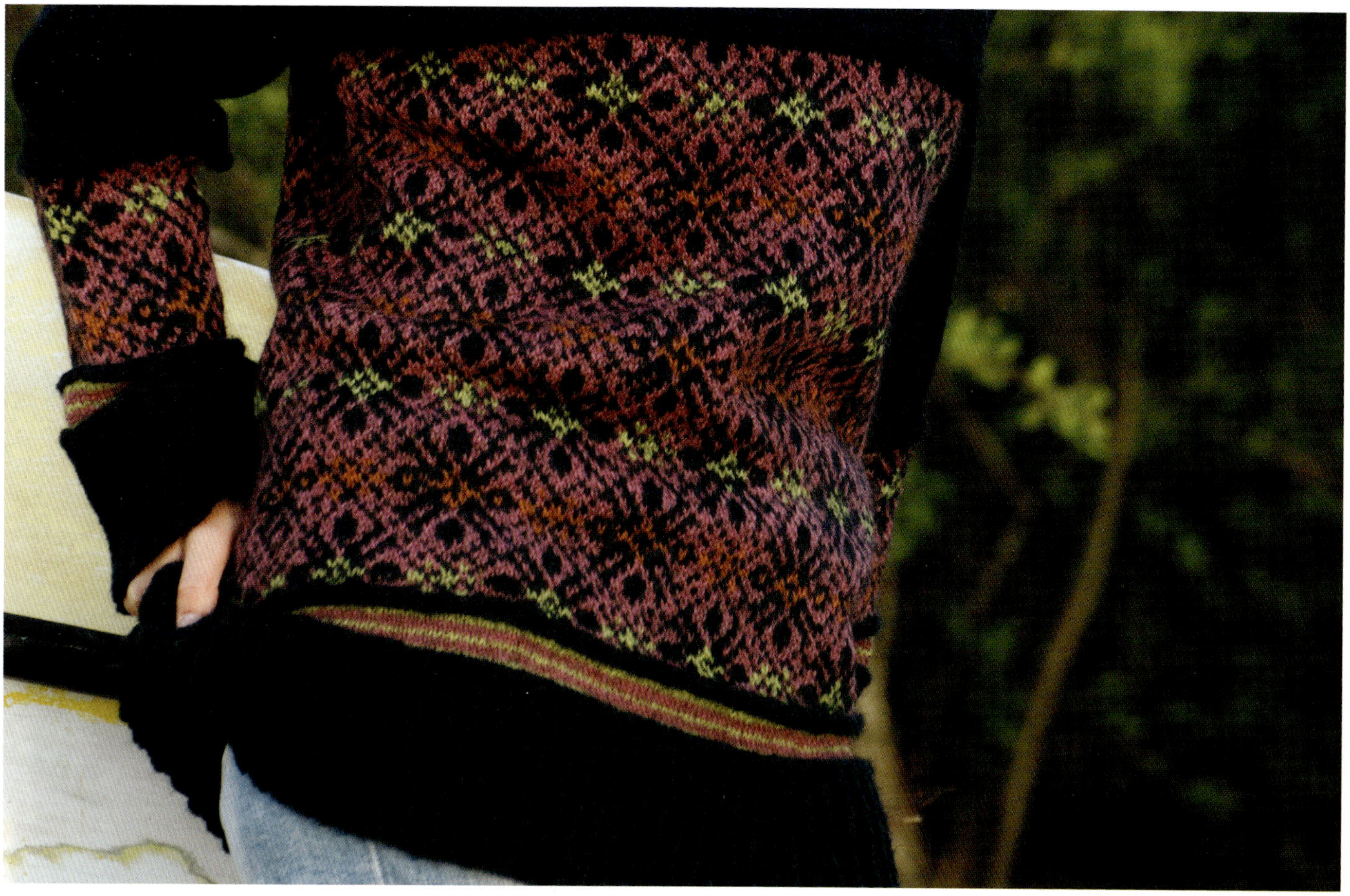

CHART

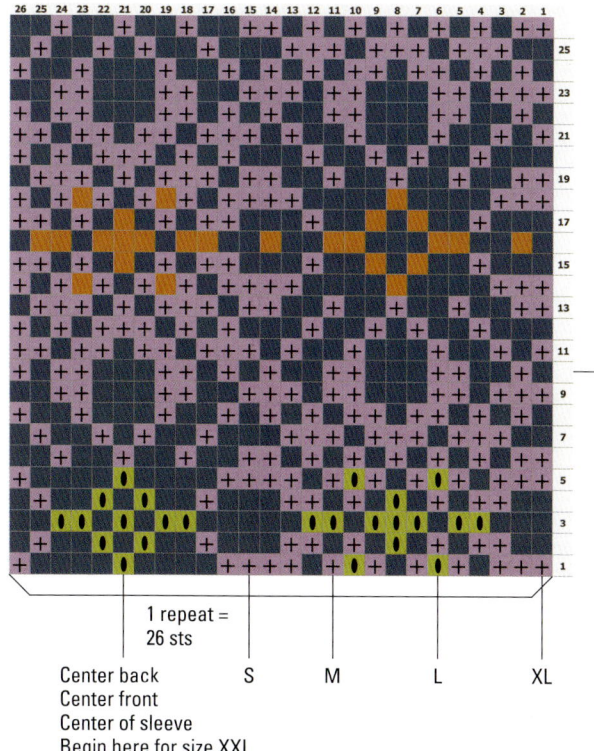

26 25 24 23 22 21 20 19 18 17 16 15 14 13 12 11 10 9 8 7 6 5 4 3 2 1
25
23
21
19
17
15
13
11
9
7
5
3
1
Begin sleeve here.
Work to end of chart
and then work Rows
1-9 of chart.
1 repeat =
26 sts
Center back
Center front
Center of sleeve
Begin here for size XXL
S
M
L
XL

Symbols Key

■	Color 1
+	Color 2
▮	Color 3
■	Color 4

LILLI

A lovely pullover with details in silver yarn. This sweater has a lace pattern on the sleeves, raglan shaping, and crocheted details in silver on each side of the lace panels on the sleeves. It's knitted in a light, soft yarn that has a little silk.

SKILL LEVEL
Intermediate to Experienced

SIZES
S (M, L, XL)

FINISHED MEASUREMENTS
Chest: 36 (38¼, 40½, 44½) in / 91 (97, 103, 113) cm
Total Length: 22¾ (23¾, 24½, 25¼) in / 58 (60, 62, 64) cm
Sleeve Length: 18½ (19, 19¼, 19¾) in / 47 (48, 49, 50) cm or desired length

MATERIALS
Yarn:
CYCA #3 (DK, light worsted) Permin Zenta (50% wool, 30% silk, 20% polyamide, 197 yd/180 m / 50 g)
and
Lurex yarn such as Concorde: CYCA #1 (fingering) Rauma Concorde (64% rayon, 36% polyester, 137 yd/ 125 m / 25 g)
Yarn Colors and Amounts:
Color 1: Zenta Natural 883322: 400 (400, 450, 500) g
Color 2: Concorde Silver 21: 25 (25, 25, 25) g
Needles: U. S. sizes 2.5 and 4 / 3 and 3.5 mm: circulars and sets of 5 dpn.
Crochet Hook: U. S. size B-1 or C-2 / 2.5 mm

GAUGE
24 sts in stockinette with larger needles = 4 x 4 in / 10 x 10 cm.
Adjust needle size to obtain correct gauge if necessary.

Garter Stitch Edging with Silver Yarn:
Rnd 1: Knit with Concorde.
Rnd 2: Purl with Concorde.
Rnd 3: Knit with Zenta.
Rnd 4: Purl with Zenta.
Rep Rnds 1-4 once more and end with knit 1 rnd with Zenta.

BODY

The body is worked in the round from the bottom up.
With smaller circular and Color 1, CO 218 (234, 246, 270) sts. Join, being careful not to twist cast-on row; pm for beginning of rnd. Work garter stitch edging with silver as described above. Pm at each side = 109 (117, 123, 135) sts each for front and back. Change to larger circular. With Color 1, continue around in stockinette until body measures 2½ (2¾, 3¼, 3½) in / 6 (7, 8, 9) cm. Decrease 1 st at each side of markers: K2tog, knit until 2 sts before side marker, k2tog tbl, sl m, k2tog. Knit until 2 sts rem, k2tog tbl = 4 sts decreased around. Decrease the same way on every 3rd rnd, 8 times. Then, work without further shaping until body measures a total of 7 (7½, 8, 8¼) in / 18 (19, 20, 21) cm. Now increase 1 st on each side of each marker = 4 sts increased around. Increase the same way on every 5th rnd, 8 times = 218 (234, 246, 270) sts. Then, continue without further shaping until body measures a total of 14½ (15, 15½, 15¾) in / 37 (38, 39, 40) cm.

Shape Armholes: BO 8 sts on each side as follows: BO 4 sts, knit until 4 sts before side marker, BO 8 sts, knit until 4 sts before marker, BO 4 sts. Set body aside while you knit sleeves.

SLEEVES

The sleeves are worked in the round from the bottom up.
With smaller dpn and Color 1, CO 53 (55, 57, 61) sts. Work garter stitch edging with silver as described above. Change to larger dpn. With Color 1, work lace panel centered on sleeve as follows: K15 (16, 17, 19), work lace following chart = 23 sts and k15 (16, 17, 19). Continue as est, and *at the same time* increase 2 sts centered on underarm on every 6th rnd until there are 89 (93, 97, 105) sts. Work new sts in stockinette. When sleeve is 18½ (19, 19¼, 19¾) in / 47 (48, 49, 50) cm long, shape armholes on next rnd: BO 4 sts, work until 4 sts rem, BO 4 sts. Set first sleeve aside while you make second sleeve the same way.

JOINING BODY AND SLEEVES

Place all pieces on larger circular: front, right sleeve, back, left sleeve = 364 (388, 408, 448) sts total. Pm at each intersection of body and sleeve = 4 markers. Knit 2 rnds without decreasing.

Raglan Shaping: Knit until 2 sts before first marker, k2tog tbl, sl m, k2tog. Decrease the same way at each marker.

Decrease as est on every rnd 5 (7, 9, 11) times and on every other rnd 26 (26, 27, 29) times = 116 (124, 120, 128) sts rem. *At the same time*, when 8 decrease rnds rem and the body is approx. 20½ (21, 21¼, 21¾) in / 52 (53, 54, 55) cm long, BO the center front 27 (29, 31, 33) sts for front neck. Now work back and forth. At each side of neck, on every other row, BO 2 sts once and 1 st 4 times. Continue raglan shaping on every RS row until all decreases have been worked and 77 (83, 77, 83) sts rem.

Neckband: Move rem 77 (83, 77, 83) sts to smaller circular and pick up and knit 8 sts on each side of neck and 27 (29, 31, 33) sts along front neck = 120 (128, 124, 132) sts. Work 1 rnd k1tbl, adjusting stitch count to 116 (120, 124, 128). Work garter stitch edging as described above. BO with Zenta.

FINISHING

Seam underarms.
Weave in all ends neatly on WS. *Gently* steam press sweater on WS under a damp pressing cloth.

Decorative Edging on Sleeves: With crochet hook and silver yarn: Work 1 row of slip sts along each of the outermost stitch rows on lace panel on each sleeve. Keep working yarn on WS as you crochet. Cut yarn and fasten off well.

Tip: Glitter yarn can easily slip out, so be sure to knot it firmly before cutting yarn.

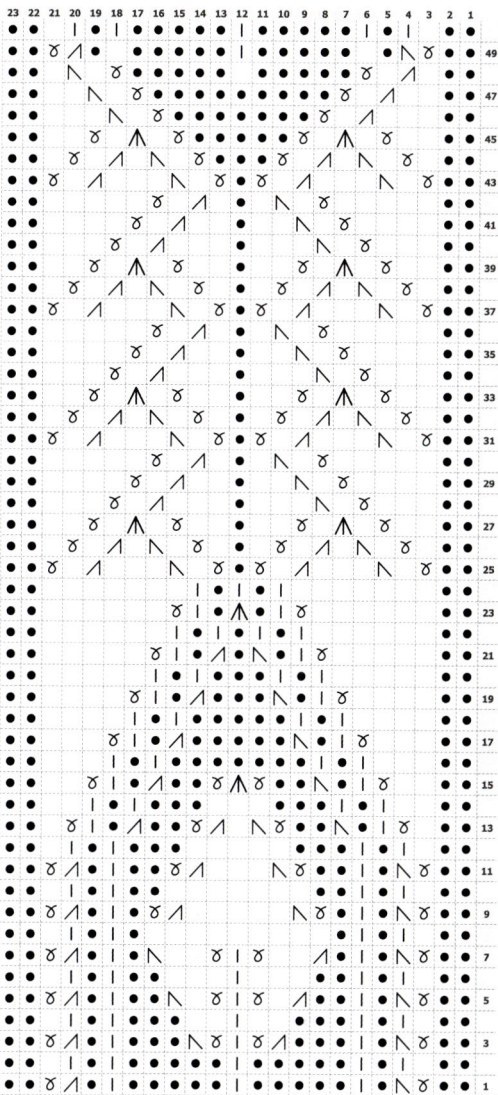

CHART

1 repeat = 23 sts

Symbols Key

☐	Knit
•	Purl
○	Yo
I	K1bl
╲	K2tog tbl
╱	K2tog
⋏	Sl 1, k2tog, psso

WINTER POETRY

A long pattern-knitted cardigan with exquisite details. The sweater has raglan shaping and knitted bands. To finish it off, it is decorated with a play of buttons and ribbon on each side of the front bands.

SKILL LEVEL
Experienced

SIZES
S (M, L, XL)

FINISHED MEASUREMENTS
Chest: 37¾ (40½, 43, 47¾) in / 96 (103, 109, 121) cm
Total Length: 29¼ (30, 30¾, 31½) in / 74 (76, 78, 80) cm
Sleeve Length: 19 (19¼, 19¾, 20) in / 48 (49, 50, 51) cm or desired length

MATERIALS
Yarn:
CYCA #3 (DK, light worsted) Du Store Alpakka Sterk (40% Merino wool, 40% alpaca, 20% polyamide, 150 yd/137 m / 50 g)

Yarn Colors and Amounts:
Color 1: Brown 824: 250 (250, 300, 300) g
Color 2: Fog Blue 848: 200 (200, 250, 250) g
Color 3: White 851: 100 (100, 100, 100) g
Color 4: Light Brown 823: 200 (200, 250, 250) g
Needles: U. S. sizes 2.5 and 4 / 3 and 3.5 mm: circulars and sets of 5 dpn.
If you work two-color stranded knitting more tightly than one-color knitting, use U. S. 6 / 4 mm for those sections.
Notions: 12 small buttons—I used 2 different metal buttons. Approx. 1.5 yd / 1.4 m ribbon for front bands

GAUGE
24 sts in stockinette/pattern with U. S. 4 / 3.5 mm or U. S. 6 / 4 mm = 4 x 4 in / 10 x 10 cm.
Adjust needle size to obtain correct gauge if necessary.

BODY

The sweater is worked in the round from the bottom up.

With smaller circular and Color 2, CO 232 (247, 262, 292) sts. Join, being careful not to twist cast-on row; pm for beginning of rnd. Work p2, k3 ribbing around, ending rnd with p2. Work around in ribbing for 1¼ in / 3 cm. Change to larger circular for stranded colorwork and work 1 rnd with Color 4 (= Row 1 of Chart I), adjusting stitch count to 233 (247, 261, 295) sts. Pm for beginning of rnd and after 6 sts = center front steek.

Steek: Purl steek sts; do not include steek sts in stitch counts. Work steek sts in a single color throughout. Count 56 (60, 63, 71) sts and pm = right front. Count 115 (121, 129, 147) sts and pm = back. The rem 56 (60, 63, 71) sts = left front. Work around in pattern following Chart I. Work the 6 steek sts, and then begin at arrow for right front. Work in pattern to side marker and then begin at arrow on back for your size. Work to next side marker and work in pattern, so left front mirror-images right front. After completing Chart I, work Chart II: Purl 6 steek sts, and then begin pattern at arrow for right front. Work in pattern to side marker and then begin at arrow on back for your size. Work to next side marker and work in pattern, so left front mirror-images right front. Complete all rows of Chart II, and then work Rows 1-5 of Chart I. Now work pattern on Chart III for rest of body. Purl steek, then begin pattern at arrow for right front. Work in pattern to side marker and then begin at arrow on back for your size. Work to next side marker and work in pattern, so left front mirror-images right front.

When body measures a total of 20 (20½, 21, 21) in / 51 (52, 53, 53) cm, shape armholes:

Shape Armholes: Knit until 4 (4, 4, 4) sts rem before marker on right front, BO 8 (8, 8, 8) sts. Knit until 4 (4, 4, 4) sts before next side marker, BO 8 (8, 8, 8) sts, knit to end of rnd. Set body aside while you knit sleeves.

SLEEVES

With smaller dpn and Color 2, CO 45 (45, 50, 55) sts. Divide sts onto dpn and join. Work in p2, k3 ribbing for 1¼ in / 3 cm. Change to larger dpn (size needed to obtain gauge for two-color knitting) and knit 1 rnd with Color 4 (= Row 1 of Chart I), adjusting stitch count to 52 (54, 56, 60) sts. Work in pattern following Chart I. See arrow for center of sleeve and count back to determine first st of rnd. Work 1 chart rep in length. *At the same time:*

Shape Sleeve: On every 8th rnd, increase 2 sts centered on underarm until there are 84 (88, 92, 98) sts. After completing Chart I pattern, work rest of sleeve following Chart III. See arrow for center of sleeve and count back to determine first st of rnd. Continue as est until sleeve is 19 (19¼, 19¾, 20) in / 48 (49, 50, 51) cm long. Make sure you end sleeve on same rnd as for body. Now shape armhole:

Shape Armhole: BO 4 (4, 4, 4) sts, knit until 4 (4, 4, 4) sts rem and BO those sts. Set first sleeve aside while you knit second sleeve the same way.

JOINING BODY AND SLEEVES

Place all pieces on circular of size needed to obtain gauge for two-color

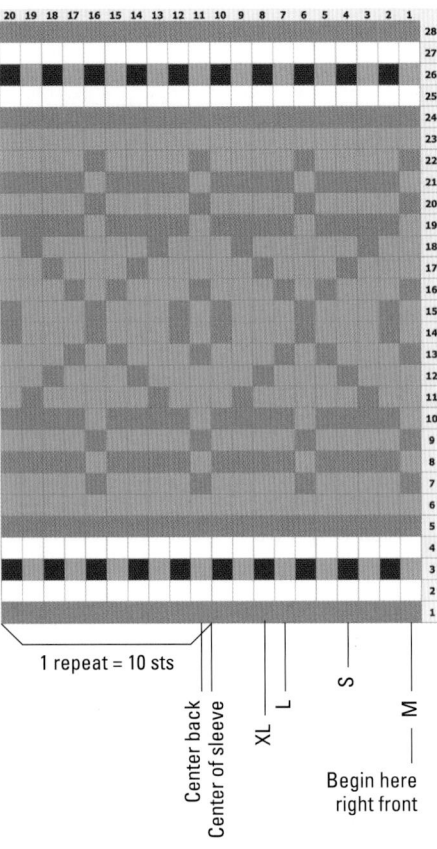

CHART I

1 repeat = 10 sts

Center back / Center of sleeve

XL

L

S

M

Begin here right front

knitting: right front, right sleeve, back, left sleeve, left front = 369 (391, 413, 459) sts total, including steek. Pm at each intersection of body and sleeve = 4 markers. Continue working pattern following Chart III, but with last st of front and first st on sleeve, k2tog with Color 1 = center st of raglan shaping. This st is always worked with Color 1; pm around st. Also join st on the other intersections between body and sleeve = 4 sts decreased around. Continue around, and *at the same time* shape raglan at all markers.

Raglan Shaping: Knit in pattern until 2 sts before raglan marker, k2tog with Color 1, knit marked st with Color 1, k2tog tbl with Color 1 = 8 sts decreased around.

Work the 6 steek sts with Color 1. Decrease the same way on every rnd 6 (8, 10, 12) times and then on every

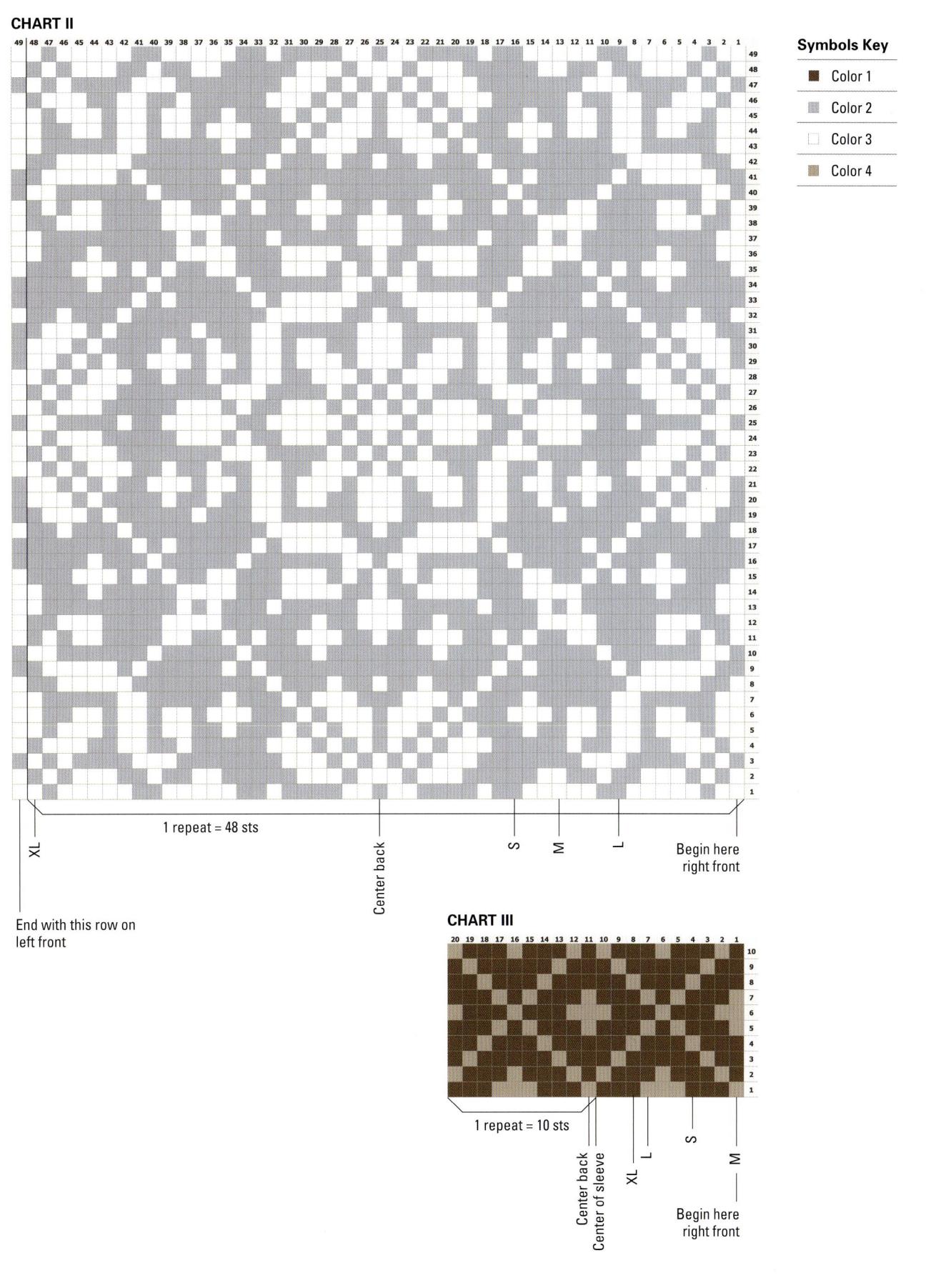

every other rnd 25 (25, 25, 28) times = 117 (123, 129, 135) sts rem. *At the same time*, when 6 raglan decrease rnds rem, BO the center 24 (26, 28, 30) sts at center front: BO the 6 steek sts, BO 9 (10, 11, 12) sts knit until 9 (10, 11, 12) sts rem and BO those sts. Now work back and forth.

Shape Neck: At each side of front neck, on every other row, BO 2 sts once and 1 st 4 times. Continue raglan shaping on every RS row. BO rem sts.

FINISHING

Seam underarms.
Weave in all ends neatly on WS. Machine-stitch 2 lines, zigzag and straight stitch, on each side of center front sts. Carefully cut open up center of steek.

Left Front Button Band: With smaller circular and Color 2, pick up and knit approx. 147 (150, 153, 155) sts along left front. Work 1 row k1tbl on WS. Work back and forth in k3tbl, p2 ribbing (on WS, work the purl sts tbl). Work 7 rows in ribbing and then knit 1 row on WS = foldline. Work 7 more rows in ribbing and then BO in ribbing. Fold band at foldline and sew down smoothly on WS to cover cut steek edge. Mark spacing for 11 buttons (the 12th button will be on the neckband).

Right Front Buttonhole Band: Work as for left front band, but make 11 buttonholes spaced to match buttons. Make buttonholes on the 3rd and 11th rows. For each buttonhole: yo, k2tog tbl. On next row, purl each yarnover.

Neckband: With smaller circular and Color 2, pick up and knit 123 (123, 128, 128) sts along neckline. Work 1 row k1tbl on WS. Work back and forth in k3tbl, p2 ribbing (on WS, work the purl sts tbl); end row with k3tbl. Work 7 rows in ribbing and then knit 1 row on WS = foldline. Work 7 more rows in ribbing and then BO in ribbing.

NOTE: On 3rd and 11th rows, make a buttonhole as before: work 3 sts, buttonhole, complete row.
Fold band at foldline and sew down smoothly on WS.
Sew buttons onto left front band spaced to match buttonholes.
Sew ribbon beside each front band.
Gently steam press sweater on WS under a damp pressing cloth.

AMANDA

A classic and timeless pattern-knitted cardigan with raglan shaping. The straight silhouette has garter stitch ridges between the body and yoke. This lovely sweater goes just as well with jeans every day as it does with nice slacks on a night out.

SKILL LEVEL
Intermediate to Experienced

SIZES
S (M, L, XL, XXL)

FINISHED MEASUREMENTS
Chest: 34¾ (37, 40¼, 44, 48¾) in / 88 (94, 102, 112, 124) cm
Total Length: 22 (22¾, 23¾, 24½, 25¼) in / 56 (58, 60, 62, 64) cm
Sleeve Length: 19 (19¼, 19¼, 19¾, 19¾) in / 48 (49, 49, 50, 50) cm

MATERIALS
Yarn:
CYCA #2 (sport, baby) Hillesvåg Ask/Hifa 2 (100% Norwegian wool, 344 yd/315 m / 100 g)
Yarn Colors and Amounts:
Color 1: Light Blue-Violet Heather 6541: 150 (150, 200, 200, 250) g
Color 2: Light Gray Heather 6054: 100 (100, 100, 150, 150) g
Color 3: Light Blue-Violet 6041: 250 (250, 300, 300, 350) g
Needles: U. S. sizes 1.5 and 2.5 / 2.5 and 3 mm: circulars and sets of 5 dpn.
If you work two-color stranded knitting more tightly than one-color knitting, use U. S. 4 / 3.5 mm for those sections.
Notions: 11 buttons to match sweater colors. Approx. 1.3 yd / 1.4 m ribbon to cover cut steek edges.

GAUGE
24 sts in stockinette pattern on larger needles = 4 x 4 in / 10 x 10 cm.
Adjust needle size to obtain correct gauge if necessary.

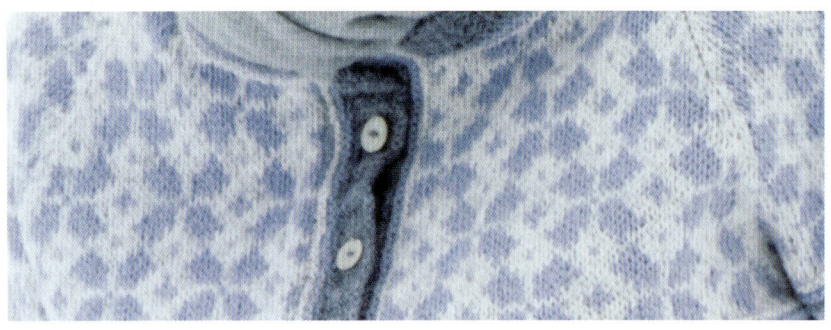

Pattern: See Charts I and II—on Chart II, the body uses Color 2 as the main color and Color 1 for the contrast. On the sleeves, Color 3 is the main color and Color 2 is the contrast.

BODY

The sweater is worked in the round from the bottom up.
With smaller circular and Color 1, CO 206 (222, 242, 266 294) sts + 6 steek sts at center front.
Steek: Purl steek sts; do not include steek sts in stitch counts. You can work the 2 center sts with contrast color if you like, to secure yarns and make it easier to cut steek open later. Join, being careful not to twist cast-on row; pm for beginning of rnd. Work 9 rnds in p2, k2 tbl ribbing, ending rnd with p2 before the steek. Knit 1 rnd, purl 1 rnd.
Change to Color 3 and knit 1 rnd, purl 1 rnd. Change to Color 2 and knit 1 rnd, purl 1 rnd. On last rnd, increase 5 (3, 3, 3, 3) sts evenly spaced around (but not in steek) = 211 (225, 245, 269, 297) sts.
Place markers: K52 (56, 60, 66, 74), pm = right front. K107 (113, 125, 137, 149); pm = back. K52 (56, 60, 66, 74 = left front. Make sure the 6 steek sts are at center front. Change to larger circular (size needed to obtain gauge for two-color knitting). Work in pattern following Chart I. See arrow for beginning st for your size. Work rep around and continue in pattern until body measures 13¾ (14¼, 14½, 15, 15½) in / 35 (36, 37, 38, 39) cm.
Shape Armholes: Knit until 4 (4, 4, 4, 4) sts rem before first side marker; BO 8 (8, 8, 8, 8) sts. Knit until 4 (4, 4, 4, 4) sts before next side marker; BO 8 (8, 8, 8, 8) sts, and then knit to end of rnd. Set body aside while you knit sleeves.

SLEEVES

With smaller dpn and Color 3, CO 52 (52, 56, 56, 60) sts. Divide sts onto dpn and join. Work 9 rnds in p2, k2 tbl ribbing. Knit 1 rnd, purl 1 rnd. Change to Color 1 and knit 1 rnd, purl 1 rnd. Change to Color 2 and knit 1 rnd, purl 1 rnd. On last rnd, increase 4 (6, 4, 6, 6) sts evenly spaced around = 56 (58, 60, 62, 66) sts. Change to larger circular (size needed to obtain gauge for two-color knitting). Work in pattern following Chart I, with Color 3 as main color and Color 2 as contrast color. See arrow for center of sleeve and count back to determine first st of rnd.
Shape Sleeve: On every 5th rnd, increase 2 sts centered on underarm until there are 90 (94, 98, 108, 116) sts. Work new sts into pattern. Continue as est until sleeve is 19 (19¼, 19¼, 19¾, 19¾) in / 48 (49, 49, 50, 50) cm long. Now shape armhole:
Shape Armhole: BO 4 (4, 4, 4, 4) sts, knit until 4 (4, 4, 4, 4) sts rem and BO those sts.
Set first sleeve aside while you knit second sleeve the same way.

JOINING BODY AND SLEEVES

Place all pieces on circular of size needed to obtain gauge in two-color knitting: right front, right sleeve, back, left sleeve, left front = 359 (381, 409, 453, 497) sts total, + 6 steek sts. Pm at each intersection of body and sleeve = 4 markers. With Color 1, knit 1 rnd, purl 1 rnd. Change to Color 3 and knit 1 rnd, purl 1 rnd. Change to Color 2 and knit 1 rnd, purl 1 rnd. Now work in pattern following Chart II.
Begin at arrow for right front and work up to first marker; count from center of sleeve to determine st for beginning sleeve. On back, begin at arrow for your size. Work second sleeve as for first and work left front to mirror-image right front. On 2nd rnd in pattern, begin raglan shaping:
Raglan Shaping: Knit in pattern until 2 sts before first marker, k2tog tbl sl m, k2tog. Decrease the same way at each marker = 8 sts decreased around.

NOTE: Work raglan sts with Color 2.
Decrease the same way on every rnd 5 (6, 7, 8, 9) times = 319 (333, 353, 389, 425) sts rem. Now, decrease on every other rnd a total of 25 (26, 27, 30, 34) times, and then on every rnd 3 times.
At the same time, when 6 raglan decrease rnds rem, BO the center 28

CHART I

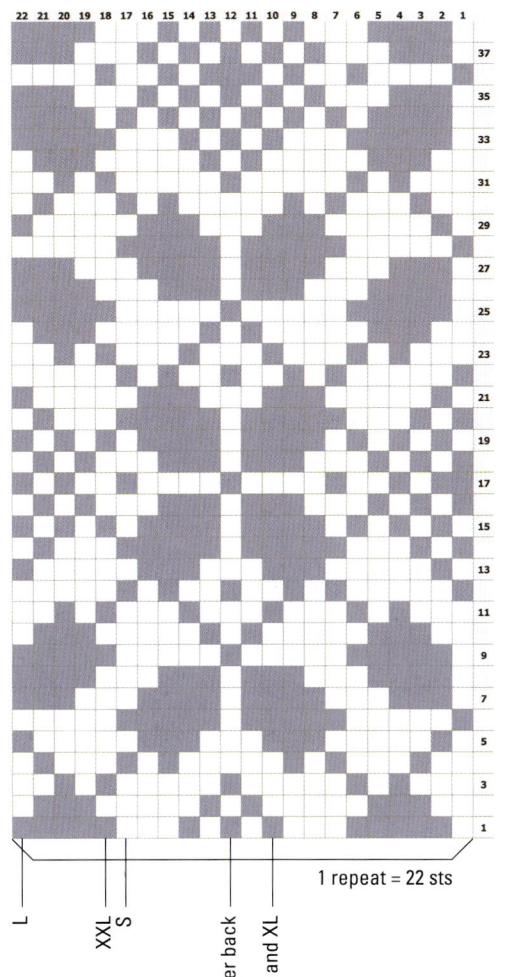

1 repeat = 22 sts

L, XXL, S, Center back, M and XL

CHART II

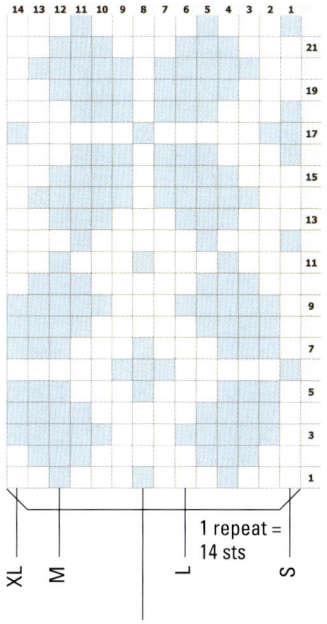

1 repeat = 14 sts

XL, M, L, S

Begin right front here
Center back and center of sleeve
XXL

Symbols Key

- ☐ Color 1 on body and Color 2 on sleeves
- ■ Color 2 on body and Color 3 on sleeves
- ▨ Color 3

(30, 32, 34, 34) sts at center front and BO the 6 steek sts = BO 14 (15, 16, 17, 17) sts on each side of steek. Now work back and forth.

Shape Neck: At each side of front neck, on every other row, BO 2 sts 2 times and 1 st 2 (2, 3, 3, 4) times. Continue raglan shaping on every RS row until all specified raglan decrease rows are finished. BO rem sts.

FINISHING

Seam underarms.
Weave in all ends neatly on WS.
Gently steam press sweater on WS under a damp pressing cloth. Machine-stitch 2 lines, zigzag and straight stitch, on each side of center front sts. Carefully cut open up center of steek.

Neckband: With smaller circular and Color 2, pick up and knit 110 (116, 120, 128, 130) sts along neckline. Work 1 row k1tbl on WS, knit 1 row. Knit 2 rows with Color 3 and knit 2 rows with Color 1. Now work p2, k2tbl ribbing (work purl sts tbl on WS) for 2¾ in / 7 cm. BO in ribbing. Fold band in half and sew down smoothly on WS.

Left Front Button Band: With smaller circular and Color 2, pick up and knit 146 (150, 154, 158, 162) sts along left front. Knit 2 rows, work 1 row k1tbl. Knit 2 rows with Color 3 and knit 2 rows with Color 1. Now work 7 rows in p2, k2tbl ribbing (on WS, work the purl sts tbl). BO in ribbing. Mark spacing for 11 buttons, with the top one ⅜ in / 1 cm below top edge and the bottom one ⅜ in / 1 cm above bottom edge.

Right Front Buttonhole Band: Work as for left front band, but on 3rd row, make 11 buttonholes spaced to match buttons. For each buttonhole: k2tog, yo twice, k2tog tbl. On next row, work each yarnover tbl in ribbing. Work 7 more rows in ribbing and then BO in ribbing.
Sew buttons onto left front band spaced as for buttonholes.
Sew ribbon on WS of each band to cover cut steek edges.

YARN RESOURCES

One must have yarn—and beautiful, soft yarn in playful colors is one of the most inspiring things I can imagine. I'm the happiest using yarn in natural materials, but sometimes the desire for a little bling arises, and then I'll choose a synthetic yarn with pretty effects such as glitter, sequins, or beads. Below you'll find information about the yarns suggested in this book. Specific yarn details are listed in each pattern.

Hillesvåg Ullvarefabrikk—www.ull.no

Ask, Sølje pelsullgarn, Tinde pelsullgarn, Vilje lamullgarn, Blåne pelsullgarn

Ask (100% Norwegian wool) is great for stranded colorwork pattern knitting and comes in more than 100 colors so you can have great color play!

Sølje pelsullgarn (100% Norwegian pelsull wool) is a light and airy wool yarn spun from Norwegian pelsull (fur sheep's wool) with heather shades of natural gray. When the wool is dyed, the pretty heather shades harmonize with each other.

Tinde pelsullgarn (100% Norwegian pellsull wool) is a slightly heavier yarn than Sølje. It is spun from Norwegian pelsull (fur sheep's wool) with heather shades of natural gray. When the wool is dyed, the pretty heather shades harmonize with each other.

Vilje lamullgarn (100% Norwegian lamb's wool) knits to the same gauge as Sølje, so these yarns can readily be combined in a project. Vilje's bright colors can't be produced in Sølje because its wool is light gray.

Blåne pelsullgarn (100% Norwegian wool) is a heavy yarn, good for outerwear and everyday, durable garments.

Du Store Alpakka—www.dustorealpakka.no

Sterk, Mini Sterk, Tynn Alpakka, Alpakka Wool, Air

Sterk (40% alpaca, 40% Merino wool, 20% nylon) is a soft, strong yarn great for pattern knitting. The yarn comes in a number of colors.

Mini Sterk (40% alpaca, 40% Merino wool, 20% nylon) is a thinner version of Sterk. It's also a soft, strong yarn, and good for pattern knitting. The yarn comes in a number of colors.

Tynn Alpakka (100% alpaca) was the first alpaca yarn we imported from Peru for Du Store Alpakka, and it introduced Norwegian knitters to alpaca. It's a super soft, lovely yarn with all the best characteristics. It works well for single-color garments.

Alpakka Wool (60% alpaca, 40% wool) knits to the same gauge as Mini Sterk and Tynn Alpakka.

Air (78% Suri alpaca, 22% polyamide/nylon) is a brushed yarn of the softest Suri alpaca that can be knitted singly or held double. It is superb when combined with other yarns.

Rowan—www.knitrowan.com

Available in the U.S. via WEBS.com, LoveCrafts.com.

Felted Tweed, Cashmere Tweed, Kidsilk Haze

Felted Tweed (50% wool, 25% alpaca, 25% viscose). I became aware of this yarn back in the 1980s when I ran the shop Colours in Oslo, and have used it continually in my work as a designer. There aren't very many tweed yarns on the market, and Felted Tweed is light and airy with colors that all harmonize with each other.

Cashmere Tweed (80% wool, 20% cashmere) is a luxury yarn with a soft blend of wool and cashmere, plus a touch of tweed effect.

Kidsilk Haze (70% mohair, 30% silk) is one of the most luscious fine mohair yarns on the market. The yarn can be worked with a single strand for super light garments, doubled, or combined with other yarns.

Strikkestua Kongsberg—now Strikk og Tøy, www.strikkogtoy.no

Amuri 4 and 8 ply

Amuri 4-ply (75% Merino wool, 25% New Zealand possum) from Naturally. Other yarns that knit to a gauge of 27 stitches in 4 in / 10 cm, such as Mini Sterk (Du Store Alpakka) can be substituted.

Amuri 8-ply (75% Merino wool, 25% New Zealand possum) from Naturally. Other yarns that knit to a gauge of 22 stitches in 4 in / 10 cm, such as Sterk (Du Store Alpakka) can be substituted.

Amuri yarn is one of my favorite yarns. It is super soft, unbelievably good for knitting with, and produces a light and lofty garment. It comes in two weights and works well for cables, lace, and pattern knitting. The yarn is produced in New Zealand, and it is uncertain how long it will be available.

Rauma Garn—www.raumagarn.no

Available in the U.S. via TheYarnGuys.com, TheWoollyThistle.com.

Plum and Concorde

Plum (70% super kid mohair, 30% nylon) is a light and lofty mohair yarn available in a large range of colors.

Concorde (36% polyester, 64% viscose) is a lurex yarn available in many colors. It provides a lovely "bling" effect on knitted garments.

ABBREVIATIONS

Permin—www.permin.dk

Angel and Zenta

Angel (70% kid mohair, 30% silk) is super soft, light, lovely mohair and silk yarn that can be knitted with one, two, or more strands held together. It is superb for knitting together with other yarns.

Zenta (50% wool, 30% silk, 20% nylon), a soft yarn that works well for garments worn indoors or in the summer when it is not too warm. It comes in many colors.

Flamingo garn og hobby—www.flamingogarn.no

Emozine from Mondial (100% wool) is a soft wool yarn with long color gradients that shift throughout each 150 g ball. It comes in many pretty color gradients.

The skirt shown on pages 20, 30, 42, 49, and 175 was knitted with Kidsilk Haze. You can find the pattern on www.karihdesign.com

BO	bind off (= UK cast off)	mm	millimeter(s)
ch	chain (crochet)	p	purl
cm	centimeter(s)	pm	place marker
CO	cast on	psso	pass slipped stitch over
dc	double crochet (= UK treble crochet)	rem	remain(s)(ing)
		rep	repeat
dpn	double-pointed needles	rnd(s)	round(s)
		RS	right side
est	established	sc	single crochet (= UK double crochet)
in	inch(es)		
k	knit	sl	slip
k2tog	knit 2 together (right-leaning decrease)	sl m	slip marker
		st(s)	stitch(es)
m	meter(s)	tbl	through back loop
M1	Make 1 increase: lift strand between two stitches onto left needle and knit into back loop to twist strand	tog	together
		WS	wrong side
		yd	yard(s)
		yo	yarnover

ACKNOWLEDGMENTS

THANK YOU TO

There are so many people to thank, but first and foremost, I want to thank Per, my most beloved work companion, critic, and cheering squad, who puts up with me when I disappear into my creative bubble and spread yarn balls, knitting needles, samples, and sketches all over the house.

A big thank you to my test knitters who have knitted samples for me for a number of years—you are invaluable.

Without models there would be no book, and these women are always ready when I ask. Thank you a thousand times over to: Maren Bømarken, Emilie Aasby Lindstadhagen, Ingrid Brandth, Caroline Støyva Eriksen, Linn Stav, Norah Sofie Sørli Thommasen, and Maren Schumann—you are all a dream to work with.

Thank you to May Britt Bjella Zamori, who reads the proofs of all my patterns—you are unique.

As usual, I have been honored to have Lise Mosveen as graphic designer for the book's interior, and this time you outdid yourself—a thousand thanks!

And last but not least, thank you to Gyldendal and Ann Kristin Nås Gjerde, my Norwegian editor, who said yes to the publication of this book.